SCOTUS 2024

Howard Schweber
Editor

SCOTUS 2024

Major Decisions and Developments of the US
Supreme Court

Editor
Howard Schweber
Madison, WI, USA

ISBN 978-3-031-78550-4   ISBN 978-3-031-78551-1   (eBook)
https://doi.org/10.1007/978-3-031-78551-1

© The Editor(s) (if applicable) and The Author(s), under exclusive license to Springer Nature Switzerland AG 2025

This work is subject to copyright. All rights are solely and exclusively licensed by the Publisher, whether the whole or part of the material is concerned, specifically the rights of translation, reprinting, reuse of illustrations, recitation, broadcasting, reproduction on microfilms or in any other physical way, and transmission or information storage and retrieval, electronic adaptation, computer software, or by similar or dissimilar methodology now known or hereafter developed.
The use of general descriptive names, registered names, trademarks, service marks, etc. in this publication does not imply, even in the absence of a specific statement, that such names are exempt from the relevant protective laws and regulations and therefore free for general use.
The publisher, the authors and the editors are safe to assume that the advice and information in this book are believed to be true and accurate at the date of publication. Neither the publisher nor the authors or the editors give a warranty, expressed or implied, with respect to the material contained herein or for any errors or omissions that may have been made. The publisher remains neutral with regard to jurisdictional claims in published maps and institutional affiliations.

Cover design by Oscar Spigolon and eStudio Calamar

This Palgrave Macmillan imprint is published by the registered company Springer Nature Switzerland AG
The registered company address is: Gewerbestrasse 11, 6330 Cham, Switzerland

If disposing of this product, please recycle the paper.

Contents

1 Introduction: The 2023–2024 Term: Is This
a "Radical" Supreme Court? 1
Howard Schweber

2 Trump V. Anderson: The Rise and Fall of Section
Three of the Fourteenth Amendment 21
Mark A. Graber

3 *Trump v. United States*: Permanent Presidential
Immunity from Criminal Prosecution 29
Evan Caminker

4 *FDA v. Alliance for Hippocratic Medicine*: Denying
Standing for Anti-Abortion Doctor Groups While
Expanding Conscience Protections 39
Susan Etta Keller

5 *Moyle v. U.S.*: Court Restores Injunction Against
Idaho Abortion Ban; Decision on the Merits Postponed 49
Leslie F. Goldstein

6 *Consumer Finance Protection Bureau v. Community
Financial Services Ass'n*: When Is an Appropriation
Not an Appropriation? 57
Chase Porter

7	*Securities and Exchange Commission v. Jarkesy*: New Limits on Administrative Adjudication William Funk	65
8	*Loper Bright v. Raimondo* and *Relentless v. Department of Commerce*: The End of *Chevron* Deference Carol Nackenoff and Avishai Greenberg	75
9	*Ohio v. Environmental Protection Agency*: The Emergency Docket Shapes National Policy Again Julie Novkov	87
10	*NetChoice* v. *Paxton*: Navigating and Refereeing Freedom of Speech in Cyberspace Mark Rush	95
11	*Murthy v. Missouri*: Jawboning, Social Media, and the First Amendment David L. Sloss	105
12	*NRA v. Vullo*: On the Line Between Government Persuasion and Government Coercion Paul E. McGreal	115
13	*Lindke v. Freed* & *O'Connor-Radcliff v. Garnier*: State Action & the First Amendment Eric T. Kasper	123
14	*United States v. Rahimi*: Setting Limits on the "Right to Bear Arms" Doni Gewirtzman	133
15	*Alexander v. South Carolina State Conference of the NAACP*: A Political Exception to the Rule Against Race-Based Redistricting Mark R. Killenbeck	141
16	*City of Grants Pass v. Johnson*, et al.: Homelessness and the Eighth Amendment William Rose	149

Index 157

List of Contributors

Evan Caminker University of Michigan Law School, Ann Arbor, USA

William Funk Lewis and Clark University, Portland, Oregon, USA

Doni Gewirtzman New York Law School, New York, NY, USA

Leslie F. Goldstein University of Delaware, Newark, Delaware, USA

Mark A. Graber University of Maryland Law School, Maryland, USA

Avishai Greenberg Swarthmore College, Swarthmore, PA, USA

Eric T. Kasper University of Wisconsin-Eau Claire, Eau Claire, WI, USA

Susan Etta Keller Western State College of Law, Irvine, CA, USA

Mark R. Killenbeck University of Arkansas School of Law, Fayetteville, NC, USA

Paul E. McGreal Creighton University School of Law, Omaha, NE, USA

Carol Nackenoff Swarthmore College, Swarthmore, PA, USA

Julie Novkov Rockefeller College of Public Affairs & Policy, University at Albany, SUNY, Albany, NY, USA

Chase Porter California Baptist University, Riverside, CA, USA

William Rose Department of Political Science, Albion College, Albion, USA

Mark Rush Washington and Lee University, Lexington, VA, USA

Howard Schweber University of Wisconsin, Madison, WI, USA; Dept. of Political Science, University of Wisconsin-Madison, Madison, USA

David L. Sloss Santa Clara University Law School, Santa Clara, CA, USA

CHAPTER 1

Introduction: The 2023–2024 Term: Is This a "Radical" Supreme Court?

Howard Schweber

Is the Roberts Court a radical Court? The answer, of course, depends on how one understands the term "radical," a term that seems to have replaced "activist" as the preferred criticism of a Court whose actions display a constitutional ideology contrary to one's own. But the term "radical" does not lack substantive meaning; rather it can be defined in multiple ways, all of which have to do with doing something different from what has been done before. A Court might be considered radical if it disregards the principle of *stare decisis* and enthusiastically overturns earlier precedents in ways other Courts might not have done. Or a Court might be radical if it is one that crafts jurisprudential principles or employs interpretive methods across a range of areas that are profoundly inconsistent with longstanding practices and understandings. Or a test for a Court's radicalism might be the potential disruptive consequence of its rulings (intended or unintended). Or "radical" might refer to a Court's

H. Schweber (✉)
University of Wisconsin, Madison, WI, USA
e-mail: howard.schweber@wisc.edu

Dept. of Political Science, University of Wisconsin-Madison, Madison, USA

© The Author(s), under exclusive license to Springer Nature Switzerland AG 2025
H. Schweber (ed.), *SCOTUS 2024*,
https://doi.org/10.1007/978-3-031-78551-1_1

assertion of authority to insert itself into areas that had previously been thought of as the business of the other branches or the States.

Or a Court could be thought of as radical if it does all four. That is the prevailing view of the Roberts Court among some of the premier legal journalists in the country.[1] Within the Court itself, accusations of radicalism have come from dissenting justices, as when Justice Sotomayor declared that the Court's decision with respect to presidential immunity "reshapes the institution of the Presidency."[2] In response, justices in the majority have accused dissenters of overreacting, as when Justice Alito referred to the issue of bans on emergency abortions as an "easy but emotional and highly politicized" question,[3] or when Chief Justice Roberts chided dissenting justices for "fear mongering on the basis of extreme hypotheticals" in response to his ruling on presidential immunity.[4] As Dahlia Lithwick points out, the language of these responses—including repeated references to "hysteria"—often seem gendered regardless of the merits of the analysis, a point that is not lost on frequently dissenting Justices Kagan, Sotomayor, and Jackson.[5] In general, the tone of this term's opinion has been marked by open hostility

---

[1] Dahlia Lithwick and Mark Joseph Stern, "The Supreme Court Is Fully MAGA-Pilled. The Time for Action Is Now or Never," *Slate.com* July 23, 2024, available at https://slate.com/news-and-politics/2024/07/supreme-court-maga-john-roberts-trump-handmaiden.html; Kate Shaw, William Baude, and Steven Vladeck, "The Justices Dropped This Bomb,' Three Legal Experts on a Shocking Supreme Court Term," *New York Times*, July 11, 2024, available at https://www.nytimes.com/2024/07/11/opinion/supreme-court-term-immunity.html; Jodie Kantor and Adam Liptak, "How Trump Shaped Supreme Court's Trump Winning Streak," *New York Times*, Sept. 15, 2024, available at https://www.nytimes.com/2024/09/15/us/justice-roberts-trump-supreme-court.html; in 2023 Linda Greenhouse argued that the Roberts Court had accomplished all five elements of a conservative strategy to remake American constitutionalism going back to the 1980s. Greenhouse, "Look at What John Roberts and His Court Have Wrought Over 18 Years," *New York Times*, July 9, 2023, available at https://www.nytimes.com/2023/07/09/opinion/supreme-court-conservative-agenda.html.

[2] *Trump v. United States*, No. 29–939, slip. op. at 1 (2024) (Sotomayor, J., dissenting).

[3] *Moyle v. United States*, No. 23–726, slip op. at 4 (Alito, J., dissenting).

[4] *Trump v. United States*, slip op. at 40 (Roberts, CJ).

[5] Dahlia Lithwick, "Don't Be Hysterical, Ladies. Daddy Chief Justice Knows Best," *Slate.com* July 03, 2024, available at https://slate.com/news-and-politics/2024/07/john-roberts-trump-immunity-sotomayor-dissent-boys-vs-girls.html.

between dissenters accusing the Court of radicalism and justices in the majority accusing dissenters of acting unreasonably.[6]

One concern with accusations of judicial radicalism is that they lead to questions about the Court's legitimacy. Chief Justice Roberts famously declared during his confirmation hearing that he considered his role to be "calling balls and strikes," an image that would be contradicted by a conclusion that he and the Court he leads are in fact pursuing an ideological vision that represents a sharp departure from long-settled understandings of basic constitutional principles. As a political matter, it is noteworthy that these accusations arise during a term in which the Court's legitimacy has separately been called into question because of a series of ethical scandals involving justices (particularly Thomas and Alito) who failed to report gifts repeatedly and over a period of years even after being made aware that the practice was problematic.[7] Whatever the particular influence of these different factors, public confidence in the Court hovered near its all-time low during the 2023–24 term.[8]

What are the merits of the claim that the Roberts Court is a radical institution? In the Introduction to *SCOTUS 2023* the editors wrote, "The rulings of June 2022 seemed to have announced nothing less than a constitutional revolution" referring to rulings that overturned *Roe v. Wade* and announced an entirely new approach to evaluating rights protected by the Due Process Clause of the Fourteenth Amendment generally; dramatically redefined Second Amendment rights and the Court's approach to rights incorporated under the Fourteenth Amendment; announced the formal adoption of the "major questions doctrine" limiting the authority of independent regulatory agencies; and substantially reduced the limitations on public school teachers imposed by the

---

[6] John Fritze, Devon Cole, Lauren Fox, "Supreme Court Strikes Down Trump-Era Ban on Bump Stocks on Guns," available at https://www.cnn.com/2024/06/14/politics/supreme-court-bump-stocks?cid=external-feeds_iluminar_yahoo.

[7] A series of reports is compiled at "Friends of the Court: Supreme Court Justices' Relationships With Billionaires," *Pro Publica*, available at https://www.propublica.org/series/supreme-court-scotus.

[8] Overall, approximately 47% of the public viewed the Court favorably. This number was highly bifurcated by party, however, with 78% of Republicans but only 24% of Democrats reporting favorable opinions. "Favorable views of Supreme Court edge up from 2023 but are still close to historic low," *Pew Research Center* August 7, 2024, available at https://www.pewresearch.org/short-reads/2024/08/08/favorable-views-of-supreme-court-remain-near-historic-low/sr_24-08-08_scotus_1/.

Establishment Clause of the First Amendment.[9] We observed, "[w]hether the developments over these two terms constitute a true constitutional revolution is open to debate. Clearly there have been deep changes, but the debate is about what those changes represent or suggest for the future." Specifically, we focused on characteristics of "incommensurability" (the extent to which new approaches are not comprehensible from the perspectives of earlier jurisprudence) and shifts in the window of what counts as "reasonable" constitutional arguments, such that new precedents are defined on the basis of arguments that would have been considered borderline or even frivolous in earlier eras, what in politics is known as the "Overton Window" of acceptable public argumentation.[10] We also identified specific patterns that would indicate an ongoing constitutional revolution

- Expansive litigation as advocacy groups test the willingness of the Court to innovate.
- New claims to standing as unusual litigants ask the Court to allow their claims.
- New constitutional doctrines with broad but uncertain implications.
- Extension of the new doctrines to unexpected areas.
- Eventual limiting principles as the Court defines the boundaries of its innovations.

What, then, have we learned from the 2023–24 term? The first three elements have been evident in full force. In the separation of powers area and the Second Amendment, earlier rulings have served as invitations to litigation for interest groups seeking to challenge longstanding understandings in both the Supreme Court and the lower federal courts.[11] As

---

[9] *Dobbs v. Jackson Women's Health Organization* (2022), *New York State Rifle and Pistol Association v. Bruen* (2022), *West Virginia v. EPA* (2022), and *Kennedy v. Bremerton School District* (2022),

[10] Hollie Clements, "The Overton Window Explained," *The Week UK*, July 30, 2019, available at https://theweek.com/102517/the-overton-window-explained; Jack Balkin, "From Off the Wall to On the Wall: How the Mandate Challenge Went Mainstream," *The Atlantic* June 4, 2012.

[11] For example, in *Aunt Bertha v. NLRB*, No. 4:24-cv-00798-P (N.D. Tex 2024) a federal judge has ruled that the adjudicatory system established under the National Labor Relations Board is unconstitutional based on the ruling in a 5th Circuit ruling that was upheld in *SEC v. Jarkesy* (see discussion, Chapt. 9 this volume). In *VanDerStok v.Garland*

the discussion above suggested, "broad but uncertain implications" are certainly at work in the rulings on presidential immunity, and "uncertainty" is the key in cases about abortion rights where the 2024 Court declined to reach questions of substantive rights. On the other hand, with regard to standing, none of the current term's cases display quite the inventiveness of the 2023 term;[12] if anything, during this term the Court has relied on standing to turn away potentially troubling cases, pushing the underlying issues to a later term for resolution, and may even have indicated a loss of patience with cause litigators bringing cases based on highly inventive theories of standing.[13] And at least in the case of Second Amendment rights we have, indeed, seen the beginning of an announcement of limiting principles, as *United States v. Rahimi* declared an outer bound (in at least one circumstance) to the extremely broad reach of Justice Thomas' analysis in *NY State Pistol and Rifle Club v. Bruen*. We also had two cases this term that simply explored areas that were essentially unknown territory: how should courts deal with an ex-president who stands accused of participating in a criminal conspiracy to overturn an election?

The one-sentence summaries and the table below provide a brief overview of the year's rulings, followed by a more detailed description of some of the dominant themes.

Summaries & Table

To summarize the year's major rulings, the Court:

---

the 5th Circuit ruled that the Supreme Court's ruling in *Bruen* required it to strike down a law banning untraceable "ghost guns"; the Supreme Court has taken up the case in its 2025 term. *VanDerStok v. Garland*, No. 23-10,718 (5th Cir. 2023).

[12] Notably, in *303 Creative v. Elenis*, 600 U.S. 570 (2023) and *Biden v. Nebraska*, 600 US 477 (2023), the Court ruled in favor of plaintiffs challenging government actions despite the lack of traditional indicia of standing. See Morgan Marietta and H. Schweber, "Introduction: the 2022–23 Term at the Supreme Court," in Marietta and Schweber eds., *SCOTUS 2023* (2024), 21–23.

[13] The Court denied *certiorari* in *Tingley v. Ferguson*, 47 F.4th 1055 (9th Cir. 2022), a First Amendment challenge to Washington state's ban on LGBTQ+ conversion therapy for minors. The case had been brought by the Alliance Defending Freedom, a religious conservative group that had previously brought cases to the Court that turned out to be based on factually questionable claims of standing.

(1) Ruled that States do not have the authority under Sect. 1.3 of the XIVth Amendment to remove a candidate convicted of felonies relating to an attempt to overturn a lawful election (*Trump v. Anderson*).
(2) Ruled that presidents have complete immunity from criminal prosecution for official acts and limited liability in other situations (*Trump v. United States*).
(3) Ruled that conservative doctors lacked standing to challenge federal rules permitting the distribution of the abortifacient drug mifepristone, while leaving the underlying question of the legal or constitutional status of the FDA regulations in questions (*FDA v. Hippocratic Alliance*).
(4) Lifted a stay on an injunction preventing the enforcement of Idaho's Total Abortion Ban without reaching the merits of the underlying question of the law's constitutionality (*Moyle v. United States*).
(5) Upheld the funding system employed for the Consumer Finance Protection Bureau against constitutional challenge arguing that funding any agency from an independent source unconstitutionally infringed on Congress' constitutional authority over appropriations (*Consumer Finance Protection Bureau v. Community Financial Services Ass'n*).
(6) Ruled that the use of administrative law judges to adjudicate disputes before the Securities and Exchange Commission is unconstitutional (*SEC v. Jarkesy*).
(7) Ruled that courts are not required to defer to executive agencies with respect to the interpretation of those agencies' legal mandates, abolishing the principle of "*Chevron* deference" (*Loper Bright v. Raimondo* and *Relentless v. Department of Commerce*).
(8) Stayed the enforcement of a rule regulating air pollution until all legal challenges were exhausted, expanding the role of the "shadow docket" in shaping the regulatory environment (and strongly hinting that the rule will eventually be overruled) (*Ohio v. EPA*).
(9) Declined to issue a substantive ruling on the question of how or when First Amendment overbreadth principles apply to the operation of social media platforms (*Netchoice v. Paxton*).

(10) Denied standing to state and private plaintiffs suing to challenge actions by federal government officials that were alleged to coerce social media platforms to limit expression in violation of the First Amendment (*Murthy v. Missouri*).
(11) Ruled that government officials' statements threatening legal actions against insurance companies if they did not sever ties with the National Rifle Association constituted coercion and therefore violated those insurance companies' First Amendment rights of association and expression (*NRA v. Vullo*).
(12) Established a test to determine when a state official's decision to bar individuals from posting content to his social media page constitutes state action subject to the First Amendment (*Lindke v. Freed* & *O'Connor-Radcliff v. Garnier*).
(13) Upheld a federal law preventing individuals who are under a domestic violence-related restraining order from purchasing guns (*United States v. Rahimi*).
(14) Upheld a North Carolina redistricting plan as not racially discriminatory based on the conclusion that race was secondary to political party identification in the design of the districts at issue (*Alexander v. NAACP*).
(15) Limited an earlier ruling about Eighth Amendment limits on criminal punishments based on "status" to allow municipalities to ban sleeping overnight outdoors and using those laws to displace homeless populations, effectively overruling an earlier 9th Circuit decision. *City of Grant's Pass v. Johnson* (Table 1.1).

(**Note: Issue** describes the broad topic at hand. **Vote** describes the majority and dissenting positions among the nine Justices. **Author (Majority)** notes the ideological grouping among the Justices. In general, the six conservative Justices are considered to be Samuel Alito (appointed by George W. Bush), Amy Coney Barrett (Trump), Neil Gorsuch (Trump), Brett Kavanaugh (Trump), Chief Justice John Roberts (George W. Bush), and Clarence Thomas (George H.W. Bush); the liberal Justices are Ketanji Brown Jackson (Biden), Elena Kagan (Obama), and Sonia Sotomayor (Obama)).

Table 1.1. 2023–2024 major cases

Ch	Case	Issue and Outcome	vote	Majority (Author)
President Trump				
1	*Trump v. Anderson*	States do not have authority to remove a candidate from a federal ballot under Sect. 1.3 of the XIVth Amendment	9–0	*Per curiam*
2	*Trump v. United States*	Presidents have absolute immunity from criminal liability for "core" official acts, and presumptively immune for official acts within the "outer perimeter" of their authority	6–3	Roberts (6 conservatives); Kagan, Sotomayor, Jackson dissenting
Abortion				
3	*FDA v. Alliance for Hippocratic Medicine*	Standing of physician denied in challenge to FDA regulations re mifepristone	9–0	Kavanaugh
4	*Moyle v. United States*	Hold on enforcement of Idaho abortion ban restored	6–3	*Per curiam*, 5 separate opinions
Federal Agency Power				
5	*Consumer Finance Protection Bureau v. Comm'ty Financial Services Ass'n*	Independent funding system for federal agency upheld	7–2	Thomas; Alito, Gorsuch, dissenting
6	*SEC v. Jarkesy*	Use of administrative law judges to adjudicate disputes before Securities and Exchange Commission ruled unconstitutional	6–3	Roberts, 6 conservatives; Kagan, Sotomayor, Jackson dissenting
7	*Loper Bright v. Raimondo*	Federal courts are not required to defer to agency interpretations of legal mandates even if agency interpretation is reasonable, overruling *Chevron USA v. National Resources Defense Council* 467 U.S. 837 (1984)	6–3	Roberts, (6 conservatives); Kagan, Sotomayor, Jackson dissenting

(continued)

Table 1.1. (continued)

Ch	Case	Issue and Outcome	vote	Majority (Author)
8	*Ohio v. EPA*	Enforcement of EPA air pollution rules stayed pending resolution of legal challenges	5–4	Gorsuch (5 conservatives); Barrett, Sotomayor, Kagan, Jackson dissenting
First Amendment				
9	*Moody v. Netchoice LLC*	On challenge to state laws limiting content moderation by platforms, case(s) remanded for further consideration of First Amendment issues	9–0	Kagan
10	*Murthy v. Missouri*	States lack standing to challenge the federal government's efforts to persuade social media providers to moderate content	6–3	Barrett (plus 5 liberals); Alito, Thomas, Gorsuch dissenting
11	*NRA v. Vullo*	State officials' threats to bring legal action against insurance companies if they fail to disassociate from the National Rifle Association would violate the First Amendment if proved	9–0	Sotomayor; Gorsuch, Jackson concurring
12	*Lindke v. Freed*	Public official excluding individuals from a private social media account does not violate the First Amendment unless the official was speaking on behalf of the government	9–0	Barrett
Second Amendment				
13	*United States v. Rahimi*	Second Amendment does not bar federal law prohibiting individuals subject to domestic violence-related restraining orders from purchasing guns	8–1	Roberts; Thomas dissenting
Race and Redistricting				

(continued)

Table 1.1. (continued)

Ch	Case	Issue and Outcome	vote	Majority (Author)
14	*Alexander v. NAACP*	North Carolina redistricting plan upheld on grounds that primary consideration was political advantage rather than race	6–3	Alito (6 conservatives); Kagan, Sotomayor, Jackson dissenting
Rights of Homeless				
15	*City of Grants Pass v. Johnson*	Banning sleeping overnight outdoors is not cruel and unusual punishment under the Eighth Amendment because it does not punish individual based on their status (homeless) but rather on the basis of their conduct	6–3	Gorsuch (6 conservatives); Kagan, Sotomayor, Jackson dissenting

Cases by Subject

President Trump (*Trump v. Anderson, Trump v. United States*).

The two cases involving ex-President Trump both explored uncharted territory. In *Trump v. Anderson,* the Court confronted the question of whether Sect. 1.3 of the XIVth Amendment grants States the authority to exclude candidates from ballots in federal elections. No judicial precedents existed on the question. The conservative justices who self-describe as originalists might have turned to the history of the textual provision and asked its original purpose understanding. As Mark Graber explains, they would have discovered that the main concern at the time of the adoption of the XIVth Amendment was to ensure that ex-Confederates would not take office, and the prevailing understanding was that States had authority to determine eligibility in elections. Nonetheless, the justices chose to eschew any serious historical analysis and instead focused on a policy question—the concern for "chaos" in elections—and delivered a ruling that completely deprived States of any authority to exclude insurrectionists from federal elections. This decision was 9–0.

In *Trump v. United States*, the Court confronted the question of a president's immunity from criminal prosecution. In *Nixon v. Fitzgerald* the Court had ruled that president do not have immunity in civil cases, but nonetheless the majority found that President Trump and all future presidents have sweeping criminal immunity including absolute immunity for "core" official acts and presumptive immunity for other official acts. The majority ruled that courts could not even hear evidence to show criminal activity if that evidence concerned official acts, an outcome more protective of presidents than almost anyone had expected. As in the case of *Trump v. Anderson*, there was no attempt by the conservative majority to present their analytical framework as grounded in any historical or textual understanding; rather they appealed to purely prudential concerns about political partisanship.

Effectively, in both cases, the Roberts Court asserted judicial authority to use separation of powers to protect the American political system from what the justices view as dangers to itself. An observer might rightly observe that these concerns were noticeably absent in other cases concerning partisan gerrymandering,[14] campaign finance contributions,[15] or congressional authority to prevent racially discriminatory "second generation" barriers to voting.[16] On the other hand, the tendency to "play political scientist"—justifying novel constitutional standards based on confident assertions of political consequences—has been a hallmark of the Roberts Court's jurisprudence of democracy.

The fact that Barrett parted from her fellow conservatives on this issue may reflect differences in life experience. The court's other conservatives spent much of their careers before becoming judges in Republican presidential administrations. In contrast, Justice Barrett grew up in Louisiana and spent almost all of her professional life in academia at Notre Dame Law School in South Bend, Ind., far from the power politics of Washington.[17] In this regard it may be noteworthy that Barrett also joined the liberal justices in dissent in *Fischer v. United States*, a decision that had the effect of dismissing prosecutions against hundreds of Jan. 6 insurrectionists.

---

[14] *Rucho v. Common Cause*

[15] *Citizens United v. FEC*, 558 U.S. 310 (2010).

[16] *Shelby County v. Holder*, 570 U.S. 529 (2013).

[17] https://www.npr.org/2024/07/02/nx-s1-5026959/supreme-court-term

Abortion (*Moyle v. United States, FDA v. Alliance for Hippocratic Care*).
Without doubt, the most notable aspect of the Court's treatment of abortion in the 2024 term was the consistent refusal to address the underlying question: after *Dobbs v. Jackson Women's Health Center*[18] what, if any, limits are there on States' authority to restrict access to abortion under federal law? That was the issue in both *FDA v. Alliance for Hippocratic Care* and *Moyle v. United States*, and in both cases the majorities sent the cases back to the lower courts without addressing the substantive issues. That does not mean, however, that these two cases do not hold implications for the future of abortion restrictions.

In *Moyle*, there were three justices (Sotomayor, Kagan, and Jackson) who wanted a ruling that the Idaho abortion ban was pre-empted by federal law. Justices Alito, Thomas, and Gorsuch wanted the Court to reach the opposite conclusion. The remaining justices, Roberts, Barrett, and Alito, focused on the question of whether a federal law that imposes conditions on spending that contradict the requirements of state law can be valid. The point is that the case's outcome leaves open a wide range of possibilities; there will unquestionably be future litigation, and the opinions in this case will provide roadmaps for litigants to tailor their arguments to appeal to particular justices.

In *FDA v. Alliance*, the Court considered a challenge under the Administrative Procedures Act to the process by which abortifacient drugs had been approved by the FDA. The challenge was brought by a group of physicians, who claimed that they would suffer "harms of conscience" from knowing that the drugs in question were being prescribed by other doctors. Rather than address the challenge directly, the justice by a vote of 9–0 declared that these plaintiffs lacked standing, overruling a decision by the Fifth Circuit that the doctors had standing *and* were likely to succeed on the merits of their claim. The grant of *certiorari* in this case seems to have been motivated by a desire to discipline the Fifth Circuit, which has lately developed a reputation for entertaining arguments that the Supreme Court finds to be implausible; the fact that the issue under consideration was standing rather than substantive abortion rights means

---

[18] See Mary Ziegler, "*Dobbs v. Jackson Women's Health Organization* on Abortion," in Morgan Marietta ed., *SCOTUS 2022* (Palgrave Macmillan 2023), Chapt. 2.

that the Supreme Court was able to send this message without saying anything about the actual regulations at issue.[19]

Federal Agency Power

If there is one area in which the Roberts Court's 2024 term is rightly described as "radical" it is this one. This may not be surprising, as restructuring the system of federal regulatory agencies has been a core element of today's conservative judicial philosophy that characterizes the majority of the Roberts Court's justices.

Loper Bright v. Raimando was by some measures one of the most "radical" decisions ever, in that it effectively overruled a staggering number of earlier decisions. The decision was also radical in that it sharply departed from well-established jurisprudence that had the support of both judicial liberals and judicial conservatives (notably Antonin Scalia). The gravamen of the majority's ruling was that courts will no longer be bound to defer to an agency's "reasonable" interpretation of its mandate under statutes passed by Congress, but will rather independently determine whether the agency's actions go beyond the correct reading of the statutory text. This ruling should be understood in combination with the decision two terms ago in *West Virginia v. EPA*[20] declaring for the first time that where "major questions" are concerned a grant of authority to an agency must be explicit. On the other hand, the question of how radical the consequences of the ruling in *Loper Bright* will be is not yet clear; it will depend on how federal judges use their new-found authority. The case was 6–3, with the Court's conservative bloc overwhelming the three more liberal justices.

Another decision with arguably even greater potential to racially alter the way government operates is *SEC v. Jarkesy*. For decades, hundreds of agencies have relied on administrative law judges who are experts in the relevant fields, presiding over specialized courts, to adjudicate claims

---

[19] See Stephen I. Vladeck, "'How the Fifth Circuit Won by Losing," *Atlantic*, July 7, 2024, available at https://www.theatlantic.com/ideas/archive/2024/07/how-fifth-circuit-won-losing/678918/, noting that 2024 is the third consecutive term in which the Court has overruled the Fifth Circuit on questions of standing.

[20] 597 U.S. 697 (2022), see R. Shep Melnick, "West Virginia v. EPA on Climate Change and Administrative Power," in Morgan Marietta ed. *SCOTUS 2022* (Palgrave Macmillan 2023), chapt. 11.

either against the government or between private parties. In *Jarkesy* the Court, for the first time, declared these "Article II courts" to be unconstitutional because they violate the VIIth Amendment's guarantee of a right to jury trial in "civil cases." If taken literally, this ruling would mean that the entire system of administrative law courts has to be abolished and replaced, presumably by the addition of hundreds of new federal judges who will be appointed through the usual highly politicized process without any guarantee of substantive expertise. Litigators are already seizing on this possibility. In the 5th Circuit, Amazon has succeeded in obtaining a stay of litigation pending resolution of its claim that the NLRB's system of adjudicating disputes is unconstitutional under *Jarkesy*[21]; many more cases challenging the structures of many more agencies can be expected. If there is a limiting principle to the *Jarkesy* rule—if *some* administrative courts are permissible in some categories of cases—it will be left to the Supreme Court to clarify those principles in final appeals of future cases. The *Jarkesy* decision, like the decision in *Loper Bright*, was 6–3.

In *EPA v. Ohio,* the Court's action was far less obviously radical; the decision was to stay the implementation of a new environmental rule pending full judicial review. In fact, however, the decision was indicative of a trend. The judicial review in question involves a determination of whether the new rules were adopted in a manner that was "arbitrary and capricious" in violation of the Administrative Procedures Act. The 5–4 majority, comprising the conservative Justices less Justice Barrett, granted the stay on the basis of their conclusion that the challenge to the adoption of the rule was likely to succeed. As the dissenters pointed out, the majority was treating the test far less deferentially than has been the decades-long tradition in APA cases. In other words, as in the *Loper Bright* and *Jarkesy* cases, the Court's dominant conservatives expanded the authority of courts to limit the independence of regulatory agencies in ways that are sharply—even "radically"—different from established judicial understandings.

In the discussion of *Jarkesy*, above, the point was raised that limiting principles that apply to a newly announced rule may appear in later cases. That is exactly what happened in *Consumer Finance Protection Bureau*

---

[21] *Amazon.com v. NLRB*, No 24050761 (5th Cir. 2024), unpublished order, available at https://aboutblaw.com/bfNa.

v. Community Finance. In 2020, the Court had ruled that the appointment and removal provisions of the law creating the Consumer Finance Protection Board were unconstitutional because they unduly limited the ability of a president to influence the policy direction taken by an independent agency.[22] In the 2024 term a new challenge was brought, this time claiming that the agency's independent funding source infringed on Congress' appropriation power. In a 7–2 opinion written by Justice Thomas, the Court rejected this challenge, indicating a limit to the scope of challenges the majority—comprising both conservatives and liberals—are likely to accept going forward. This is consistent with a pattern that has been repeatedly observed with respect to the Roberts Court; a new rule with potentially enormous consequences is announced with very little detailed explanation. The decision announcing the rule serves as an invitation to litigation, leaving the lower federal courts the task of trying out different theories, and then when those cases reach the Supreme Court a limiting principle is or is not adopted…years after the original ruling.

First Amendment Freedom of Speech

The Court's treatment of freedom of speech cases is in some ways the exact opposite of its treatment of cases involving agency powers. In a series of three cases, the Court in 2024 considered questions of how First Amendment principles should apply to social media, and in all three the majority's conclusion was that there is no need for new principles while declining to reach the substantive issues in the cases before them.

In *Moody v. Netchoice LLC*, a challenge to state laws that sought to limit the ability of social media platforms to moderate their content was remanded (sent back to the lower court) with the slightly astonishing observation that none of the parties had explored the First Amendment issues involved in the case, particularly the application of free speech principles to non-state actors. In *Murthy v. Missouri*, a challenge brought by states and private parties to the federal government's efforts to persuade social media platforms to limit misinformation was dismissed for lack of standing. Both these cases had received the required four votes for *certiorari*, both asserted novel theories of the First Amendment in response to new challenges posed by social media, and neither case resulted in a ruling

---

[22] See H. Schweber *Seila Law Firm LLC v. CFPB* on Separation of Powers," in Morgan Marietta ed., *SCOTUS 2020* (Palgrave MacMillan 2021), Chapt. 13.

on any First Amendment issues. *Lindke v. Freed* also involved social media, in this case a government official who had banned individuals from access to his private account. Again, this case invited the Court to adopt a new principle: that the distinction between personal and professional expression by government officials is different in the context of social media than in more traditional contexts. And again, the Court declined to adopt a new rule, instead applying traditional standards to conclude that there is no First Amendment issue unless the official in question is speaking in his or her professional capacity as a government representative.

Finally, in *NRA v. Vulllo*, the Court considered the line between persuasion and coercion in the context of claims that New York State officials had threatened insurance companies with retaliatory actions unless they disassociated themselves from the National Rifle Association. As in the other First Amendment cases, the Court declined to adopt any new principles, instead determining that if proven at trial such threats would constitute violations of the insurance companies' First Amendment rights of speech and association.

Only *Murthy* was decided 6–3; the other three cases were all 9–0. In *Murthy,* the dissenters—Alito, Thomas, and Gorsuch—wanted the Court to reach the question of whether the Biden administration's actions had reached the level of a First Amendment violation. Even if that question had been reached, however, there is no clear way to predict what the answer would have been.

Second Amendment

In the discussion of agency powers, above, the point was made that sometimes a radical new rule is announced with very little explication, and then its limiting principles appear later after additional cases have worked their way through the lower courts. This is exactly what happened in *United States v. Rahimi*. In 2020, Justice Thomas wrote an opinion for a 6–3 majority that completely upended existing Second Amendment jurisprudence in *New York Rifle and Pistol Club v. Bruen*.[23] In *Bruen*, Thomas announced that no regulations of guns would be considered constitutional unless it could be shown that analogous restrictions existed circa 1787. In *Rahimi*, however, all the other justices joined together (8–1,

---

[23] See Douglas Dow, "*New York Rifle and Pistol v. Bruen* on the Second Amendment and Concealed Carry Laws" in Morgan Marietta ed., *SCOTUS 2022* (Palgrave MacMillan 2023), chapt. 11.

Thomas dissenting) to rule that the analogy need not be exact, and on that basis upheld the constitutionality of a federal law prohibiting individuals under domestic violence-related restraining order from purchasing firearms.

Race and Redistricting

The Roberts Court has a long-established pattern of ruling in ways that weaken the reach of the Voting Rights Act of 1965 and the XIVth and XVth Amendment provisions it enforces, starting with *Shelby County v. Holder*.[24] In *Alexander v. NAACP* the Court continued this pattern, ruling that a North Carolina redistricting plan that used race as a proxy for political partisanship (because of racialized voting patterns in which African-American voters usually vote for Democrats) should not be understood as racially discriminatory. The Roberts Court had already ruled that political gerrymandering raises no constitutional problems.[25] The conclusion in *Alexander* simply put racial gerrymanders motivated by political considerations into the category of partisan rather than racial district-drawing. The decision was 6–3, with the conservative supermajority voting as a bloc, an outcome that demonstrates the continuing ideological divide over a doctrinal development that was radical when it began and is now being played out to its logical conclusions with no clear limiting principle emerging. What was a radical development in 2013 looks like a continuing trend that has not yet reached its end ten years later.

Rights of Homeless People

In *City of Grant's Pass v. Johnson*, the Court considered the question of what limits the Constitution sets on municipalities' attempts to deal with homeless populations on their streets. In an earlier era, "vagrancy" laws had permitted the police to arrest someone for nothing more than lacking a visible purpose in walking down a street. Starting in 1972, these laws were struck down as void for vagueness; the extreme discretion

---

[24] 570 U.S. 529 (2013).
[25] See Carol Nackenoff and Abigail Diebold, "*Rucho v. Common Cause* on Partisan Gerrymandering and the Political Question Doctrine," in Morgan Marietta ed., *SCOTUS 2019* (Palgrave Macmillan 2020).

granted to police to arrest whomever they wanted meant that individuals had no adequate notice of what conduct was or was not illegal. In 2018, the Ninth Circuit in *Martin v. City of Boise* ruled that punishing people who were involuntarily homeless violated the VIIIth Amendment's ban on cruel and unusual punishment because it meant punishing people merely for their status rather than their voluntary conduct.[26] The majority, in an opinion by Justice Gorsuch, overruled *Martin* without explicitly saying so by holding that the constitutional ban on punishing individuals based on their status has to be applied very narrowly. Gorsuch focused on the claim that at least some of the homeless persons involved in the cases refused to enter shelters—meaning they were not "involuntarily" homeless—and on the point that sleeping outdoors names a conduct, not a "status." In dissent, Justice Sotomayor pointed to the record of City Council proceedings that she argued showed that the real goal of the statute was precisely to drive homeless people out of the city. Gorsuch and the majority, however, took a more formalistic approach, focusing on the reference in the text to conduct (sleeping outdoors) and declining to inquire further. Gorsuch also noted that similar statutes exist in municipalities all over the country, perhaps indicating a concern with the possible (radical?) consequences of reaching a conclusion that such laws are barred by the Constitution.

Conclusion: Was the 2024 Roberts Court "Radical"?

The answer to the question that has framed this discussion is mixed. It is difficult to deny that in the areas of agency authority the 2024 term saw genuinely radical changes in the law, whether one measures that concept in terms of precedents overturned, degree of departure from earlier jurisprudence that was thought to be settled, policy consequences, or implicit claims about the proper role of courts. On the other hand, in the abortion cases, the Court declined to explore the possible implications of its earlier rulings, insisting on further development of arguments in lower court cases or cases featuring different parties. In the Second

---

[26] *Martin v. City of Boise*, 902 F.3d 1031 (9th Cir. 2017); see also *Robinson v. California*, 370 U.S. 660 (1962) (striking down a law making it a crime to be a drug addict).

Amendment area, the Court announced a principle limiting the potential radical consequences of one of its most controversial earlier rulings, while in the area of race-based redistricting the conservative supermajority did the opposite, extending the at-the-time-radical implications of earlier cases. In the First Amendment area, the majority of the Court insisted that there is no need for new doctrine at all, only the application of traditional rules to new settings ... while sending the most difficult inquiries back to the lower courts for further discussion. How to view these results is in the eye of the observer: one might reasonably say that the 2024 term Roberts Court was radical only in certain areas, or one might with equally reasonableness say that the same Court was only *not* radical in certain areas.

CHAPTER 2

Trump V. Anderson: The Rise and Fall of Section Three of the Fourteenth Amendment

Mark A. Graber

Section Three of the Fourteenth Amendment went on a rollercoaster ride in the third decade of the twenty-first sentence. That provision declares:

> No person shall be a Senator or Representative in Congress, or elector of President and Vice-President, or hold any office, civil or military under the United States, or under any State, who, having previously taken an oath, as a member of Congress, or as an officer of the United States, or as a member of any State legislature, or as an executive or judicial officer of any State, to support the Constitution of the United States, shall have engaged in insurrection or rebellion against the same, or given aid or comfort to the enemies thereof. But Congress may be a vote of two-thirds of each House, remove such disability.

M. A. Graber (✉)
University of Maryland Law School, Maryland, USA
e-mail: mgraber@umaryland.edu

© The Author(s), under exclusive license to Springer Nature Switzerland AG 2025
H. Schweber (ed.), *SCOTUS 2024*,
https://doi.org/10.1007/978-3-031-78551-1_2

Section Three from the end of Reconstruction to the end of the Trump presidency was prominently invoked to disqualify a person from federal or state office only once, when Congress in 1920 concluded that the Socialist Victor Berger, by opposing World War One, had given aid and comfort to the enemies of the United States that rendered him ineligible to sit in the House of Representatives.[1] On or about January 1, 2021, I finished a chapter for a book in the *Forgotten Fourteenth Amendment*[2] series the first sentence of which was "Section Three is the most forgotten provision of the forgotten Fourteenth Amendment." The next week, on January 6, 2021, an insurrection occurred on congressional grounds.

Several past and present government officials, most notably then President Donald Trump, allegedly participated in the events of January 6 in some form. Section Three became hot stuff. As one of the handful of people who at the time knew anything about Section Three,[3] I made a number of media appearances, wrote numerous short pieces,[4] and participated in the campaign to disqualify Donald Trump including serving as an expert witness in a Section three case in New Mexico.[5] Then in 2024, the Supreme Court in *Trump v. Anderson*[6] ruled that state courts could not disqualify candidates for the presidency and that candidates for the presidency could be disqualified only in pursuance of congressional legislation approved by federal courts. Within two weeks, the media requests

---

[1] See Myles S. Lynch, "Disloyalty & Disqualification: Reconstructing Sect. 3 of the Fourteenth Amendment," 30 *William & Mary Bill of Rights Journal* 153, 210–214 (2021).

[2] The first volume was published in 2023. See Mark A. Graber, *Punish Treason, Reward Loyalty: The Forgotten Goals of Constitutional Reform after the Civil War* (University Press of Kansas: Lawrence, 2023).

[3] See especially, Gerard Magliocca, "Amnesty and Section Three of the Fourteenth Amendment," 36 *Constitutional Commentary* 87, (2021).

[4] Most notably, I crossed a major item off my bucket list by placing an opinion piece in *The New York Times*. Mark A. Graber, "Donald Trump and the Jefferson Davis Problem," *The New York Times*, November 29, 2023, https://www.nytimes.com/2023/11/29/opinion/trump-president-candidate-constitution.html.

[5] I advised the Committee for Responsibility and Ethics in Washington, that brought the litigation that culminated in *Trump v. Anderson*, wrote amicus briefs for the Supreme Court of the United States, the Supreme Court of Colorado, and the Maine Secretary of State, and served as an expert witness at the hearing that resulted in the Sect. 3 disqualification of Couy Griffin, a county commissioner in New Mexico.

[6] 601 U.S. 100 (2024).

and opportunities had dried up and Section Three returned to its former obscurity, unlikely to be invoked again once the memory of January 6 fades.

The substantive case for disqualifying Donald Trump is simple, particularly from an originalist perspective.[7] Common and constitutional law when Section Three of the Fourteenth Amendment was ratified treated an insurrection as an assemblage of persons resisting any federal law by force or intimidation for a public purpose. The mob on January 6, 2021, satisfied all those criteria: it was an assemblage (more than one person); that assemblage was resisting the federal laws governing the peaceful transition of federal power; force and intimidation were involved in the attacks on police officers (as well as with nooses with the vice president's name); and the purpose of the resistance was to achieve the public goal of maintaining Donald Trump in power. Common and constitutional law when the Fourteenth Amendment was ratified regarded any person who knowingly participated in any facet of an insurrection as having engaged in that insurrection. Donald Trump incited his supporters to violently attack Congress and made no effort to curb the violence once started. Every court that reached the merits concluded that the attack on the Capitol was an insurrection.[8] Every state court that reached the merits prior to the Supreme Court's ruling in *Trump v. Anderson* concluded that Donald Trump participated in that insurrection,[9] and there was no

---

[7] The arguments for the conclusions developed in this paragraph are set out in Mark A. Graber, "Section Three of the Fourteenth Amendment: Insurrection," ___ *William and Mary Bill of Rights Journal* ___ (2024). For contrary arguments, see Josh Blackman and Seth Barrett Tillman, "Sweeping and Forcing the President into Sect. 3," 28 *Texas Law and Politics* 350 (2024); Kurt Lash, "The Meaning and Ambiguity of Section Three of the Fourteenth Amendment," 47 *Harvard Journal of Law and Public Policy* ___ (2024).

[8] See *Anderson v. Griswold*, 543 P.3d 283, 342 (Colo. 2023), *rev'd*, 601 U.S. 100 (2024) *Anderson v. Trump*, 2024 COEL 000013, 2024 Ill. Cir. LEXIS 1, at *22–23 (Ill. Cir. Ct. Feb. 28, 2024);); Ruling of the Secretary of State, ME 32–33 (Dec. 28, 2023), https://www.maine.gov/sos/news/2023/Decision%20in%20Challenge%20to%20Trump%20Presidential%20Primary%20Petitions.pdf [https://perma.cc/S8GC-HZNF].

[9] See *Anderson v. Griswold*, 543 P.3d 283, 342 (Colo. 2023), *rev'd*, 601 U.S. 100 (2024) *Anderson v. Trump*, 2024 COEL 000013, 2024 Ill. Cir. LEXIS 1, at *22–23 (Ill. Cir. Ct. Feb. 28, 2024);); Ruling of the Secretary of State, ME 32–33 (Dec. 28, 2023), https://www.maine.gov/sos/news/2023/Decision%20in%20Challenge%20to%20Trump%20Presidential%20Primary%20Petitions.pdf [https://perma.cc/S8GC-HZNF].

plausible reason for the Supreme Court to reach a different conclusion. Or so we maintained.

No good procedural reasons existed for failing to disqualify what the concurrence in *Trump v. Anderson* referred to as an "oathbreaking insurrectionist."[10] The historical evidence clearly indicated that Section Three was intended to cover all insurrections, not merely the insurrections involved in what some drafts of Section Three declared to be "the late rebellion."[11] The members of the Thirty-Ninth Congress who drafted Section Three spoke of the president as an officer of the United States and an officer under the United States, and the presidency as an office of the United States and an office under the United States. Presidents and members of Congress routinely spoke of the presidential oath of office as an oath to support the Constitution. Other provisions of the Reconstruction Amendments are self-enforcing, they may be enforced by federal and state courts in the absence of federal legislation. If federal legislation were deemed necessary to enforce the Thirteenth Amendment and Section 1 of the Fourteenth Amendment, then the constitutional ban on slavery did not legally end human bondage and *Brown v. Board of Education*[12] was wrongly decided. No historical or textual reason existed to treat differently Section 3 of the Fourteenth Amendment. Or so we maintained.

Litigation to enforce Section Three initially enjoyed some success when state courts reached the merits of the disqualification issue—several state courts claimed that state law prohibited state courts from disqualifying candidates for the presidential office during the party primary season.[13] A local court in New Mexico disqualified a county commissioner who participated in the January 6 insurrection.[14] The Supreme Court of Colorado endorsed all elements of the substantive and procedural case against Trump when disqualifying him from the state ballot in the 2014

---

[10] *Trump v. Amderson*, at 118 (Sotomayor, Kagan, and Jackson, JJ., concurring).

[11] *Congressional Globe*, 39th Cong., 1st Sess., p. 2287.

[12] 347 U.D. 483 (1954).

[13] *Davis v. Wayne County Election Commission*, ___ N.W.2d ___, 2023 WL 8656163, *16 (Mich. App. 2023); *Growe v. Simon*, 997 N.W.2d 81, (Minn. 2023).

[14] *State ex rel. White v. Griffin*, No. D-101-CV-2022–00473, slip op. (N.M. Santa Fe Jud. Dist. Sept. 6, 2022).

national election.[15] Several weeks later the Secretary of State in Maine reached the same conclusion,[16] as did, a few months later, a local court in Illinois.[17]

The Supreme Court reached a different conclusion. From the beginning of deliberations, *The New York Times* reported, Chief Justice John Roberts was determined to reverse decisions keeping Trump off state ballots.[18] That Roberts and the other justices quickly reached this conclusion, while perhaps injudicious, would not be surprising in a case involving the Commerce Clause, free speech, or other matter that is frequently litigated before the Supreme Court. What made the brief deliberations in *Trump v. Anderson* remarkable is the insistence that states could not disqualify candidates for the presidency at a time when it was unclear whether any member of the Court had any prior familiarity with Section Three of the Fourteenth Amendment at all.

Having determined (or predetermined) that states should not disqualify presidential candidates who participated in the January 6, 2024 insurrection, the Supreme Court issued a brief, unanimous unsigned opinion that appears to have been written by the Chief Justice.[19] The *per curiam* opinion began with federalism, asserting that "the Fourteenth Amendment restricts state power,"[20] and that "Section 3 of the Amendment likewise restricts state autonomy."[21] The justices noted that states could not disqualify insurrectionists before the Civil War and that Section Three "does not affirmatively delegate… to the States"[22] the power to prevent candidates for federal office from being on the state election ballot. Doing so would violate federalism. The *per curiam* opinion

---

[15] *Anderson v. Griswold*, 543 P.3d 283 (Colo. 2023).

[16] *State of Maine Secretary of State, Ruling of the Secretary of State* (Dec. 28, 2023), https://www.maine.gov/sos/news/2023/Decision%20in%20Challenge%20to%20Trump%20Presidential%20Primary%20Petitions.pdf; *see also* H.R. Rep. No. 117–663 (2022).

[17] *Anderson v. Trump*, No. 2024 COEL 000013, 2024 Ill. Cir. LEXIS 1, at *36 (Ill. Cir. Ct. Feb. 28, 2024).

[18] Jodi Kantor and Adam Liptak, "How Roberts Shaped Trump's Supreme Court Winning Streak," *The New York Times*, September 15, 2024.

[19] Jodi Kantor and Adam Liptak, "How Roberts Shaped Trump's Supreme Court Winning Streak," *The New York Times*, September 15, 2024.

[20] *Id.* at 109 (majority opinion).

[21] *Id.* at 108.

[22] *Anderson*, at 111.

insisted, "the Constitution guarantees the entire independence of the General Government from any control by the respective States."[23]

Section 3 was also found not to be "self-executing," meaning that federal legislation would be required before the provision could be enforced. A crucial passage in *Trump v. Anderson* claimed that Reconstruction Republicans maintained, "[t]he Constitution 'provide[d] no means for enforcing' the disqualification, necessitating a 'bill to give effect to the fundamental law embraced in the Constitution.'"[24] Congress could disqualify, however, only under the watchful eyes of the Supreme Court. "Any congressional legislation enforcing Section 3 must," the Court insisted, "reflect 'congruence and proportionality' between preventing or remedying that conduct and the means adopted to that end."[25]

Justice Amy Coney Barrett's opinion pointed out that all nine justices agreed that states could not disqualify candidates for the presidential office.[26] She would have gone no further. Her concurrence futilely asked the court to be a voice of unity in a time of social division. "The Court has settled a political charged issue in the volatile season of a Presidential election," she wrote. "Particularly in this circumstance, writings on the Court should turn the national temperature down, not up."[27]

Justices Sonia Sotomayor, Elena Kagan, and Ketanji Brown Jackson were less willing to be good sports about the perceived excesses of the majority opinion. They supported the *per curiam* view that state disqualification threatened "a chaotic state-by-state patchwork, at odds with our Nation's federalism principles."[28] On the other hand, the concurrences rejected the idea that congressional legislation was a prerequisite to Section 3's disqualification provision. "Nothing," the three more liberal justices pointed out, "in that unequivocal bar suggests that implementing

---

[23] *Trump v. Anderson*, at 111.

[24] *Trump v. Anderson*, 601 U.S. at 110 (emphasis added). This sentence was edited in ways that would earn an undergraduate an F. What Trumbull actually said was "[t]he Constitution provides no means for enforcing itself, and this is merely a bill to give effect to the fundamental law embraced in the Constitution." *Congressional Globe*, 41st Cong., 1st Sess., p. 626.

[25] *Trump v. Anderson*, at 115.

[26] *Trump v. Anderson*, at 117–118 (Barrett, J., concurring).

[27] *Trump v. Anderson*, at 118 (Barrett, J., concurring).

[28] *Trump v. Anderson*, at 119 (Sotomayor, Kagan, and Jackson, JJ., concurring).

legislation enacted under Section 5 is 'critical.'"[29] In addition, the majority's reading of Section Three undercut that provision's vesting Congress with the power to forgive past insurrectionists. "It is hard to understand why the Constitution would require a congressional supermajority to remove a disqualification if a simple majority could nullify Section 3's operation by repealing or declining to pass implementing legislation."[30] Insisting on legislation to implement Section Three made that provision an anomaly in federal constitutional law, given that every other provision of the Fourteenth Amendment and every other presidential qualification can be enforced directly by the federal judiciary. *Trump v. Anderson*, the concurrence concluded, "simply creates a special rule for the insurrection disability in Section Three."[31] The only issue the concurrence left open is why the above considerations do *not* also justify state disqualifications, which are no more barred by the text of Section Three than federal judicial disqualifications.

A different Supreme Court majority might have made a more powerful case that states should not have the constitutional power to disqualify candidates for the national executive. A fair case can be made that the national government ought to make the rules for national elections, and that states can no more be trusted to tax the national bank fairly than to fairly assess the qualification of national candidates.[32] Whether such an argument is available to the Roberts Court is doubtful, however. Past precedents that *Trump v. Anderson* left standing permit states to regulate elections in ways that may prevent candidates for the presidency from appearing on the state ballot.[33] Justice Neil Gorsuch while on the lower federal courts did not quake when states disqualified presidential candidates for being underage. "[A] state's legitimate interest in protecting the integrity and practical functioning of the political process," he stated, "permits it to exclude from the ballot candidates who are constitutionally

---

[29] *Trump v. Amderson*, at 121 (Sotomayor, Kagan, and Jackson, JJ., concurring).

[30] *Trump v. Amderson*, at 121 (Sotomayor, Kagan, and Jackson, JJ., concurring).

[31] *Trump v. Amderson*, at 122 (Sotomayor, Kagan, and Jackson, JJ., concurring).

[32] See Neil S. Siegel, "Narrow But Deep: The *McCulloch* Principle: Collective Action Theory, and Section Three Enforcement," 39 *Constitutional Commentary* (forthcoming 2024).

[33] *Storer v. Brown*, 415 U.S. 724 (1974); *Jenness v. Fortson*, 403 U.S. 431 (1971).

prohibited from assuming office."[34] *Trump v. Anderson* gave no good reason why states could be trusted to implement the presidential qualifications outlined in Article II but not the presidential qualification added in Section Three of the Fourteenth Amendment.

The Fall and Winter law reviews may be the last hurrah for Section Three. Commentary on *Trump v. Anderson* is more likely to be read as memoirs by historians than as sources of law by litigators. Section 3 will be relevant again only in the unlikely event that Trump wins the presidency in the 2024 national election and Democrats gain control of both Houses of Congress. Perhaps one or two minor officials may keep a few of us occupied, but most participants in the attempt to disqualify Donald Trump have gotten back to our day jobs. Our return to obscurity is likely good for the country. A constitutional democracy that depends on constitutional litigation to keep oath breaking insurrectionists out of office in the long run is not likely to remain a constitutional democracy.

---

[34] Hassan v. Colorado, 495 F. App'x 947, 948 (10th Cir. 2012). See Socialist Workers Party of Illinois v. Ogilvie, 357 F. Supp. 109 (N.D. Ill. Sept. 21, 1972).

CHAPTER 3

Trump v. United States: Permanent Presidential Immunity from Criminal Prosecution

Evan Caminker

Trump v. United States accentuates the Supreme Court's recent penchant for exalting presidential power by insulating it from congressional and judicial oversight.

In 2023, Donald Trump became the first former President to face criminal prosecution for alleged misconduct during office. His indictment charged that, after losing his reelection bid in November 2020, Trump violated various federal statutes by conspiring to overturn the election's outcome by falsely claiming election fraud and interfering with the reporting, counting, and certifying of the electoral college vote. Trump moved to dismiss the prosecution, asserting immunity from criminal liability. And his claim was largely successful.

Official immunity comes in two flavors, temporary and permanent. Temporary immunity protects a president from judicial process while

E. Caminker (✉)
University of Michigan Law School, Ann Arbor, USA
e-mail: caminker@umich.edu

in office. The Court has decided that sitting presidents lack temporary immunity from civil litigation but hinted, though not yet ruled, that they enjoy temporary immunity from criminal prosecution.

Four decades ago in *Nixon v. Fitzgerald*, the Court held 5–4 that presidents enjoy permanent immunity from civil suits seeking monetary damages for acts taken during office that lie "within the outer perimeter of [their] official responsibility."[1] The Court observed that presidents make "sensitive and far-reaching decisions" about "matters likely to arouse the most intense feelings," and they need "the maximum ability to deal fearlessly and impartially with" their duties. But damages liability might make them "unduly cautious in the discharge of [their] official duties," afraid of being sued by people incidentally injured by their decisions.[2]

The Court, however, suggested this reasoning might not support criminal immunity, where prosecution vindicates the public interest and decisions are made by accountable prosecutors checked by independent grand juries rather than by self-interested private citizens. As Justice White observed in dissent, the "contention that the President is immune from criminal prosecution" is not "credible"[3]—an observation coming a decade after President Gerald Ford pardoned former President Richard Nixon for potential Watergate crimes, assuming no such immunity existed. And in 2021, Trump defended himself against impeachment for subverting the election by assuring that "[a] President who left office is not in any way above the law; as the Constitution states he or she is like any other citizen and can be tried in a court of law."[4] At that point, it was "widely assumed that Presidents lack a corresponding permanent immunity from criminal liability and sanctions."[5]

---

[1] 457 U.S. 731, 756 (1982).

[2] *Ibid.* at 752 & n.32.

[3] *Ibid.* at 780.

[4] 2 Proceedings of the U.S. Senate in the Impeachment Trial of Donald John Trump, S. Doc. 117-2, p. 144 (2021).

[5] Evan Caminker, "Democracy, Distrust, and Presidential Immunities," 36 Constitutional Commentary 255, 267 (2021).

The Supreme Court's Pro-Immunity Reasoning

Today's Supreme Court sees things differently. In a 6–3 decision, authored by Chief Justice Roberts and joined by the other five Republican-appointed (including three Trump-appointed) Justices, the Court concluded that "the nature of Presidential power requires that a former President have some immunity from criminal prosecution for official acts during his tenure in office."[6] The Court described this immunity's broad contours, but it left much undecided and directed the district court to figure out what, precisely, remains prosecutable from the election subversion indictment.

The Court announced different rules for three categories of presidential conduct. Presidents enjoy absolute immunity when exercising "core" constitutional powers; at least-presumptive immunity when exercising non- "core" executive powers; and no immunity for "private conduct."

1. "Core" constitutional powers are those assigned to the president "conclusively" (meaning she has the last word) and "preclusively" (meaning Congress may not constrain her discretion).[7] The Court described five core powers: granting pardons, vetoing bills, removing subordinate officers, recognizing foreign governments, and investigating and prosecuting crimes. Only the first two are vested by constitutional text, with the others at best implied (interestingly, the Court omitted other textual powers such as appointing officers and being commander-in-chief). Congress "may not criminalize" exercising these "conclusive and preclusive" powers.[8]

The Court offered one example regarding Trump's indictment: he is absolutely immune from prosecution for allegedly "leverag[ing] the Justice Department's power and authority to convince certain States to replace their legitimate electors with Trump's fraudulent slates of electors," in part by encouraging the department to falsely report election fraud and threatening to replace the Acting Attorney General for refusing.[9] The Court characterized both "decid[ing] which crimes to

---

[6] Trump majority at 6.

[7] *Ibid.* at 7.

[8] *Ibid.* at 9.

[9] *Ibid.* at 19.

investigate and prosecute" and "remov[ing] the most important of his subordinates" as uncriminalizable core powers.[10]

2. A president exercises non-"core" powers when she "acts pursuant to an express or implied authorization of Congress" or acts within a "zone of twilight" where the two branches "have concurrent authority."[11] Most presidential conduct lies here, making this perhaps the most important category going forward. The Court doubled down on the concerns expressed in *Fitzgerald* concerning civil damages liability, affirming the importance of "energetic, vigorous, decisive, and speedy execution of the laws" and the president's need to have "maximum ability to deal fearlessly and impartially with the duties of his office."[12] And the criminal context amplified its concerns over chilling: "Although the President might be exposed to fewer criminal prosecutions than the range of civil damages suits that might be brought by various plaintiffs, the threat of trial, judgment, and imprisonment is a far greater deterrent."[13] Therefore, "[a] President inclined to take one course of action based on the public interest may instead opt for another, apprehensive that criminal penalties may befall him upon his departure from office," thereby "significantly undermin[ing]" her independence.[14]

The Court downplayed the protected value of "the Justice Department's longstanding commitment to the impartial enforcement of the law," as well as the protections offered by grand juries, defendants' procedural rights, and the requirement of proof beyond a reasonable doubt.[15] These protections "fail to account for the President's unique position in the constitutional scheme" and might not sufficiently mitigate the chilling effect.[16] Notably, the Court did not revisit *Fitzgerald*'s acknowledgment of a broader public interest in deterring criminal than tortious misconduct.

Given these concerns, the Court announced "at least a presumptive immunity from criminal prosecution for a President's [non-core official]

---

[10] *Ibid.* at 20.
[11] *Ibid.* at 9.
[12] *Ibid.* at 10.
[13] *Ibid.* at 13.
[14] *Ibid.*
[15] *Ibid.* at 36.
[16] *Ibid.* at 37.

acts" and noted that it might, in the future, upgrade that immunity from "presumptive" to "absolute."[17] For now, the president enjoys immunity for non-core official acts "unless the Government can show that applying a criminal prohibition to that act would pose no dangers of intrusion on the authority and functions of the Executive Branch."[18] It's unclear how to show "no dangers of intrusion" given that, by definition, some official conduct is being regulated; perhaps "intrusion" entails some notion of magnitude.

The Court preliminarily explored one example within this category, considering the charge that Trump conspired "to enlist the Vice President to use his ceremonial role at the January 6 certification proceeding to fraudulently alter the election results" by "pressur[ing] [him] to reject States' legitimate electoral votes or send them back to state legislatures for review."[19] On one hand, the Vice President may "serve as one of the President's closest advisers" and "perform[] important functions at the will and as the representative of the President."[20] So whenever they "discuss their official responsibilities, they engage in official conduct."[21] On the other hand, the Vice President presides over electoral vote certification "in his capacity as President of the Senate," and not as "an executive branch function."[22] So perhaps investigating the two leaders' communications "concerning the certification proceeding does not pose dangers of intrusion on the authority and functions of the Executive Branch."[23] Reminding lower court judges that "[i]t is ultimately the Government's burden to rebut the presumption of immunity," the Court remanded this question to the district court to assess in the first instance.[24]

3. Acts that lie beyond the "outer perimeter of his official responsibilities," or "manifestly or palpably beyond [his] authority," are unofficial.[25]

---

[17] *Ibid*. at 14.
[18] *Ibid*.
[19] *Ibid*. at 21.
[20] *Ibid*. at 22.
[21] *Ibid*. at 23.
[22] *Ibid*.
[23] *Ibid*. at 24.
[24] *Ibid*.
[25] *Ibid*. at 17.

Such acts warrant no immunity because, in general, the fear of prosecution and liability for personal acts should not chill official activity. But the Court announced three rules that narrow this pathway to holding presidents accountable. First, courts may not "deem an action unofficial merely because it allegedly violates a generally applicable law.... Otherwise, Presidents would be subject to trial on every allegation that an action was unlawful, depriving immunity of its intended effect."[26] Second, "[i]n dividing official from unofficial conduct, courts may not inquire into the President's motives" because that "would risk exposing even the most obvious instances of official conduct to judicial examination on the mere allegation of improper purpose, thereby intruding on the Article II interests that immunity seeks to protect."[27] So the government cannot argue that a presidential act (say, ordering the Secret Service to assault a rally protestor) is unofficial by alleging a personal motive (say, to rev up the crowd). And third, even when prosecuting an unofficial act, the government may not introduce evidence stemming from official acts to help prove the unofficial act. For example, this evidentiary privilege means that the government may not use "evidence concerning [Trump's] official acts" to prove "his knowledge or notice of the falsity of his election-fraud claims."[28] The Court apparently worried that a president's "decisionmaking will be distorted" by fear that official activities could provide evidence supporting unofficial crimes.[29] (Justice Barrett, who joined the rest of the Court's opinion, did not endorse this evidentiary privilege. And it remains unclear whether the privilege would similarly exclude official-acts evidence even during prosecutions of other people.) So although unofficial conduct remains non-immunized, the Court established guardrails making it more difficult to prove conduct was unofficial—and then more difficult still to prove unofficial conduct was criminal.

The Court preliminarily explored whether some other indicted misconduct qualifies as non-core official acts or unofficial acts. For example, the Court considered the "allegations regarding Trump's conduct in connection with the events of January 6 itself," including his tweets inviting

---

[26] *Ibid.* at 18–19.
[27] *Ibid.* at 18.
[28] *Ibid.* at 30–31.
[29] *Ibid.* at 31.

supporters to rally in D.C. that day and his public speech "direct[ing] the crowd ... to go to the Capitol to pressure the Vice President" after which the crowd eventually "broke into the building."[30] On one hand, "most of a President's public communications are likely to fall comfortably within the outer perimeter of his official responsibilities" because "a long-recognized aspect of Presidential power is using the office's 'bully pulpit' to persuade Americans, including by speaking forcefully or critically, in ways that the President believes would advance the public interest."[31] On the other hand, there may "be contexts in which the President ... speaks in an unofficial capacity—perhaps as a candidate for office or party leader."[32] Acknowledging that "there is not always a clear line between [the President's] personal and official affairs" and drawing one "may prove to be challenging," the Court left the initial decision to the district court upon remand.[33]

Dialogue with Dissents

Justice Sotomayor (joined by Justices Kagan and Jackson) and Justice Jackson penned ringing dissents, expressing "fear for our democracy" and concerns for "risks [that] are intolerable, unwarranted, and plainly antithetical to bedrock constitutional norms."[34]

Besides criticizing the Court's "misguided" justifications for extending permanent immunity to the criminal realm,[35] the dissenters assailed the

---

[30] *Ibid.* at 28, 29.

[31] *Ibid.* at 29.

[32] *Ibid.*

[33] *Ibid.*

[34] Sotomayor dissent at 30; Jackson dissent at 22.

[35] Justice Sotomayor's primary dissent clearly rejects, as being "as bad as it sounds" and "baseless," the notion of "expansive immunity for all official act[s]." Sotomayor dissent at 3. And it clearly rejects the new evidentiary privilege as "nonsensical." *Ibid.* Its position on absolute immunity for the exercise of core powers, however, is more tentative. The dissent concedes that "[t]he idea of a narrow core immunity might have some intuitive appeal, in a case that actually presented the issue." *Ibid.* at 23. The dissent merely objects here that Trump was not charged for anything that could conceivably be considered "core" powers, *ibid.*, and claims that the Court "expands the 'core and preclusive' category beyond recognition." *Ibid.* at 24. So the dissenting Justices leave open the possibility of endorsing a criminal immunity defense that protects a narrower set of core powers not implicated by these facts.

Court for "mak[ing] a mockery of the principle, foundational to our Constitution and system of Government, that no man is above the law."[36] In response, the Court described this "rhetorically chilling contention [a]s wholly unjustified."[37] With respect to personal misconduct, the president is "[l]ike everyone else"; and with respect to official misconduct, the president is "unlike anyone else" because "the Constitution vests in him sweeping powers and duties" and therefore immunity "does not place him above the law" but rather "preserves the basic structure of the Constitution from which that law derives."[38]

The dissents also described a parade of horribles: "When [the president] uses his official powers in any way, under the majority's reasoning, he now will be insulated from criminal prosecution. Orders the Navy's Seal Team 6 to assassinate a political rival? Immune. Organizes a military coup to hold onto power? Immune. Takes a bribe in exchange for a pardon? Immune. Immune, immune, immune."[39] In response, the Court protested that the dissents "strike a tone of chilling doom that is wholly disproportionate to what the Court actually does today."[40] But the Court did not deny that the hypothesized assassination or coup would be immunized—and recall that neither illegality nor motives may be considered when classifying conduct. (The Court did suggest in a footnote that a pardon-based bribe could still be prosecuted, but its explanation of why that would not constitute a challenge to the exercise of core powers based on its motive was somewhat unclear.) That the Court generally dismissed rather than carefully engaged with the dissents' concerns leaves unclear whether, if and when the doctrine is clarified by future rulings, the dissents' fears will be realized or their warnings will be heeded.

Methods and Motives

Three aspects of the Court's reasoning are noteworthy. First, although the six Justices forming the majority repeatedly profess fidelity to the Constitution's text and original meaning, this decision does neither. As Justice

---

[36] *Ibid.* at 1.
[37] Majority at 39.
[38] *Ibid.* at 40.
[39] Sotomayor dissent at 29–30.
[40] Majority at 37.

Sotomayor's dissent notes, "the Framers clearly knew how to provide for immunity from prosecution." They provided Congress a narrow "Speech or Debate Clause" immunity, and they knew "some state constitutions at the time of the Framing specifically provided express criminal immunities to sitting governors." Yet they "chose not to include similar language in the Constitution to immunize the President."[41] Moreover, "[t]he historical evidence that exists on Presidential immunity from criminal prosecution cuts decisively against it."[42] In response, the Court simply referred to *Fitzgerald*'s grant of civil damages immunity and explained that "[a] specific textual basis has not been considered a prerequisite to the recognition of immunity." In any event, Article II's "vesting [of] the Executive power solely in the President" supports the decision's basic separation of powers-based principles.[43] Thus, the professed textualist and originalist majority endorsed a "functionally mandated" immunity for consequentialist ends.[44]

Second, the decision reflects a particular take on the divisive nature of partisan politics today. One might worry that a sitting president has incentives to cross the line into criminal activity where doing so would appreciably advance her view of the nation's interests or her personal interests. And one might be comforted that a president also has an incentive not to prosecute her predecessors based on partisan motives, to avoid inviting her own later prosecution. The Court, however, downplays the former and rejects the latter by predicting that, absent immunity, a sitting president might well act on partisan motives and unjustifiably go after former presidents. Specifically, the Court fears that an immunized sitting president will "feel[] empowered to violate federal criminal law" less than the "more likely prospect of an Executive Branch that cannibalizes itself, with each successive President free to prosecute his predecessors, yet unable to boldly and fearlessly carry out his duties for fear that he may be next."[45] In other words, "[w]ithout immunity, such types of prosecutions of ex-Presidents could quickly become routine" thus "enfeebling"

---

[41] Sotomayor dissent at 5.
[42] *Ibid.* at 6.
[43] Majority at 37, 38.
[44] *Ibid.* at 10.
[45] *Ibid.* at 40.

the presidency.⁴⁶ This assessment appears to reflect the majority's take on our contemporary partisan environment. The Watergate era, when the nation predominantly rallied around the rule of law, seems quaint.

Third, in *Fitzgerald*, the Court specifically recognized permanent damages immunity "in the absence of explicit affirmative action by Congress," suggesting the result might change "if Congress expressly [creates] a damages action against the President."⁴⁷ Here, the Court opened no such door—perhaps reflecting a concern for partisan motives within the congressional branch as well.

As written, the Court's opinion appears more sweeping and president-protective than even Trump's most ardent supporters reasonably expected. But because the Court left important questions of application for further consideration, the decision's ultimate contours remain to be carved. And after Trump was reelected in November 2024, the prosecution was dropped without further district court development of the immunity issues. Here's hoping that future presidents will refrain from apparent criminal activity so that courts need not continue to revisit this thicket.

---

⁴⁶ *Ibid.*
⁴⁷ 457 U.S. at 748 n.27.

CHAPTER 4

FDA v. Alliance for Hippocratic Medicine: Denying Standing for Anti-Abortion Doctor Groups While Expanding Conscience Protections

Susan Etta Keller

The case of FDA v. Alliance for Hippocratic Medicine was brought by a coalition of conservative medical doctors to challenge several decisions by the Food and Drug Administration (FDA) to approve and expand access to mifepristone, one of the two drugs used in combination to accomplish most medical abortions. With a unanimous decision by the Supreme Court, proponents of reproductive rights breathed a sigh of relief, while cautioning that the ultimate fate of access to the drug is far from secure. Both the eight-justice majority opinion, authored by Justice Kavanaugh, and Justice Thomas's concurrence addressed solely the threshold question of whether the associations bringing the challenge and the doctors they represented had standing to bring the claim in the first place. In deciding

S. E. Keller (✉)
Western State College of Law, Irvine, CA, USA
e-mail: skeller@wsulaw.edu

that there was no standing, the majority left for another time a consideration of the merits of the challenge to the FDA's decisions to update the prescribing parameters and ease of access for the drug.

The doctrine of standing limits the constitutional challenges that parties can bring against both statutes and regulatory actions to those in which the plaintiffs have "a personal stake" in the outcome.[1] Normally, standing requires plaintiffs to establish some "injury in fact" that has either been caused or will be caused by the operation of the statute or regulation. Earlier, the Fifth Circuit Court of Appeals had upheld the district court's determination that organizations representing anti-abortion doctors had standing to challenge the FDA's authority to regulate a drug these doctors had no intention of ever taking or prescribing themselves. When doing so, the sympathy with which that court addressed the concerns of the anti-choice doctors suggested an ideological impetus for standing that some predicted would also animate conservative members of the Supreme Court. However, positions on standing previously staked out by Justice Thomas and other conservative justices in earlier abortion cases seem to have prevented these justices from taking an approach to standing as generous as that of the Fifth Circuit. The Supreme Court's current unwillingness to recognize the claims from these plaintiffs hardly forecloses the success of further efforts to limit the availability of mifepristone, however, either in further litigation with different plaintiffs or through other avenues the majority opinion winks at. At the same time, the most significant effect on reproductive rights by the majority opinion in *Alliance* may have been accomplished through a sleight of hand, in which the majority rests its rejection of the plaintiff's standing claims on a significantly expanded interpretation of federal conscience protection statutes that shield objecting medical care providers from participation in abortion care.

THE FIFTH CIRCUIT DECISION

The Alliance plaintiffs claimed that changes in the FDA's prescribing parameters for mifepristone, including the availability of telehealth prescriptions, meant that a greater number of pregnant people taking the

---

[1] *Food & Drug Admin. v. Alliance. for Hippocratic Med.*, 602 U.S. 367, 379 (2024).

drug would have adverse effects, including the possibility of an incomplete abortion. However, none of the plaintiffs were patients who had suffered such negative effects, nor even physicians who had such patients under their direct care. As the Supreme Court's majority decision states, standing is "substantially more difficult to establish" when the government's action hurts "someone else."[2] The Fifth Circuit was able to overcome this difficulty by finding two main kinds of potential harms to the objecting anti-abortion doctors: First, as emergency room doctors, they might be required to complete an abortion in someone suffering these alleged additional side effects, in conflict with their moral beliefs and at considerable personal distress. Second, that treating such additional patients would interfere with their practice by diverting resources and imposing increased liability and insurance costs.[3]

The sympathy the Fifth Circuit displayed toward the doctor plaintiffs for these hypothetical injuries stands in sharp contrast to the lack of regard for the impact on pregnant people if such medications were more limited. The prospect of treating affected patients "imposes considerable mental and emotional stress on emergency-room doctors," the Fifth Circuit opinion maintained, because of the "regret" and "trauma" the doctors claim such patients sometimes experience, and which would impact these concerned physicians "by extension."[4] As the Supreme Court subsequently found, both the conscience and financial harms alleged are sufficiently "speculative" and "attenuated"[5] that the causal link between challenged action and alleged harm needed for standing fails. The Fifth Circuit opinion is notable for its efforts to overcome the speculative quality of these potential injuries by using non-conditional verbs. Instead of writing that the doctors might in the future experience certain harms, the opinion manipulated the verb tense to suggest that these harms are already occurring: "The Doctors therefore *sustain* a

---

[2] *Alliance*, 602 U.S. at 382.
[3] *Alliance*, 78 F. 4th 210, 228–229 (5th cir. 2023).
[4] *Id.* at 232.
[5] *Alliance*, 602 U.S. at 369.

concrete injury *when*..."⁶ This use of language made the standing claim seem more convincing than it actually was.

Having found standing, the Fifth Circuit further found that the plaintiffs were likely to prevail in their claims that several actions by the FDA with respect to mifepristone were arbitrary, capricious, or an abuse of discretion under the Administrative Procedure Act (APA). While finding that the attacks on the initial approval of mifepristone in 2000 were time-barred, the Fifth Circuit held that plaintiffs were likely to prevail with respect to FDA actions in 2016 and 2021 that expanded access. The Fifth Circuit held that the cumulative effect of 2016 amendments increasing the gestational age at which a patient could have mifepristone prescribed, expanding prescribing powers to non-physicians, reducing follow-up appointments, and changing reporting requirements had not been properly studied or explained in the FDA's decision, rendering that decision "likely arbitrary and capricious."⁷ Similarly, it held that a set of 2021 decisions to eliminate the in-person prescribing requirement had also not been adequately studied, thus also likely violating the APA.⁸ These findings, which the Supreme Court did not address, are likely to return to the courts for consideration if more suitable plaintiffs with better standing are found to make the same claims.

STANDING IN OTHER ABORTION CASES

While rejecting the standing claims of the plaintiffs as too tenuous, the Supreme Court majority in *Alliance* would allow some types of third-party standing cases to proceed.⁹ Justice Thomas concurred separately in order to note his disagreement with third party standing in its entirety, a position that he has primarily articulated in earlier decisions concerning abortion rights. It is this previous position that appears to have prevented

---

⁶ See, e.g., *Alliance*, 78 F. 4th 210, 235 (5th cir. 2023) ("The Doctors therefore sustain a concrete injury when they are forced to divert time and resources away from their regular patients."); *Id*. at 236 ("...[T]he Doctors therefore sustain a concrete injury when mifepristone patients expose them to greater liability and increased insurance costs.").

⁷ *Id*. at 246.

⁸ *Id*. at 251.

⁹ To succeed in such cases, "the plaintiff must show that the third parties will likely react in predictable ways that in turn will likely injure the plaintiffs." Alliance at 10 (internal quotation marks omitted).

Justice Thomas and other conservative members of the court from joining any opinion that would allow the *Alliance* case to reach the merits, no matter their ideological sympathy with the plaintiffs. In his dissenting opinion in an earlier case, *June Medical, LLC* (2020), Thomas had maintained that doctors did not have standing to challenge state laws that restricted abortion rights. According to Thomas, those doctors "seek to vindicate no private rights of their own."[10] Writing separate dissents in *June Medical*, Justices Gorsuch and Alito also questioned the availability of standing for the doctors challenging abortion restrictions.[11]

In his *Alliance* concurrence, Thomas presents the claims of the anti-abortion plaintiffs as the legal equivalent of the *June Medical* claimants: "So, just as abortionists lack standing to assert the rights of their clients, doctors who oppose abortion cannot vicariously assert the rights of their patients."[12] While creating a legal equivalency, Thomas's language choices hardly create a mirror image between the two sets of plaintiffs. Indeed, he paints the *June Medical* plaintiffs as the evil twins of those in *Alliance*: the doctors favoring abortion rights are cast as "abortionists" with "clients," while those opposing abortion rights are accorded the dignity of being "doctors" with "patients." This rhetorical maneuver, however, mischaracterizes the much stronger claim to standing made by the *June Medical* plaintiffs compared to the *Alliance* plaintiffs. The *June Medical* plaintiffs had a regular practice that included patients who would be directly affected by the new restrictions on doctors' admitting privileges,[13] while the *Alliance* plaintiffs' "patients" remain speculative figures of the doctors' imagination.

By drawing this false parallel, where the plaintiffs with the stronger claim are rhetorically painted as identical legally and inferior culturally, Thomas seems to signal as best he can his ideological support for the

---

[10] *June Med. Servs. L.L.C. v. Russo*, 591 U.S. 299, 359 (Thomas, J., dissenting) (2020).

[11] *June Med. Servs. L.L.C.*, 591 U.S. at 415 (Gorsuch, J., dissenting) (2020) (arguing that standing is not available because of a lack of a close relationship between the plaintiffs and the patients they treat, and the potential for a conflict of interest); *June Med. Servs. L.L.C. v. Russo*, 591 U.S. 299, 378 (Alito, J., dissenting) (2020).

[12] *Alliance*, 602 U.S. at 398, Thomas, J. concurring.

[13] In addition, the *June Medical* plaintiffs were themselves directly affected by the restriction on their ability to provide care in the absence of the required hospital admitting privileges. The majority opinion in June Medical did not reach these questions of standing, because it deemed the standing claim to have been waived earlier in the appeals process.

Alliance plaintiff's claims, while seeking to ensure that the claims of those seeking to expand reproductive rights remain similarly constrained by limited standing rules.

Conscience Protection

Perhaps the most significant impact of the *Alliance* decision on reproductive rights lies in the majority's characterization of the scope of federal conscience protections. That characterization expands the scope considerably compared to how it is defined in federal regulations and earlier cases. Federal conscience protections for doctors who are morally opposed to abortion have been codified in a number of statutes, including the Church Amendments cited by the majority, which protect doctors who refuse to participate in abortion care from punishment or employment discrimination.[14]

To arrive at this expansion, the majority first declares that government statutes or regulations that would require doctors "to provide medical treatment against their consciences" can form the basis of a "concrete injury" necessary for standing.[15] The reason such injuries are unavailing for the plaintiffs in *Alliance* is that the plaintiffs are unable to establish that any member of their organization has been or will be faced with such an injury, because "the plaintiff doctors have not shown that they could be forced to participate in an abortion or provide abortion-related medical treatment over their conscience objections."[16] Not only does the record reflect no occasion on which any plaintiff has been required in the past to perform such services over a properly articulated objection, but the majority asserts that such an occasion is also not likely to happen in the future because of how expansive these federal conscience protections are. Relying on assertions made by the Solicitor General in response to questioning at oral argument, the majority maintains that "doctors cannot be required to treat mifepristone complications in any way that would violate the doctors' consciences."[17] Again relying on the Solicitor General's assurances, the majority describes the coverage of these protections

---

[14] *Alliance*, 602 U.S. at 387.
[15] *Id.*
[16] *Id.*
[17] *Id.* at 388.

as "broad,"[18] and further declares that "strong protection for conscience remains true even in a so-called healthcare desert, where other doctors are not readily available."[19]

The breadth of the conscience protection coverage the *Alliance* majority describes seems to contradict limitations previously placed on the exercise of these protections in both regulations and case law. Indeed, disagreement about the breadth of these protections has been a political football amid the changing of presidential administrations since 2008, as each administration has sought to revise the implementing regulations within the Department of Health and Human Services to either broaden or contract their scope in line with the political leanings of the administration. For example, the latest iteration of the relevant rules finalized prior to the *Alliance* decision in 2024 refers to a balance of interests nowhere reflected in the *Alliance* majority's characterization:

> [T]he Federal health care conscience protection statutes represent Congress' attempt to strike a careful balance between the rights of both providers and patients, and the Department intends to respect that balance.[20]

The reference to balance in the recent regulations is in part responsive to federal court decisions that struck down the Trump administration's earlier attempt to craft a rule more favorable to conscience protections. The problem the courts found with the rule promulgated by the Trump administration in 2019 was, in part, its refusal to acknowledge "undue hardship" on the healthcare entity as a countervailing factor to the need to protect individual doctors.[21] In one case, the court specifically found that the relevant legislative history for the conscience protections indicated a lack of congressional intent for the objections by individual doctors to override healthcare emergency situations.[22]

Serving as the primary justification for the dismissal of the *Alliance* case for lack of standing, these new assertions of broad conscience protections

---

[18] *Id.* at 389.

[19] *Id.* at 388.

[20] 89 Fed. Reg. 2088 (Jan. 11, 2024).

[21] *New York v. United States HHS*, 414 F. Supp. 3d 475, 504 (NYSD 2019).

[22] *New York v. United States HHS*, 414 F. Supp. 3d 475, 538 (NYSD 2019).

operate as more than dicta. By ignoring the regulatory and case history and instead purporting to merely describe an existing state of affairs that substantially expands conscience protections, the majority opinion appears to make new law in a cloaked fashion. Any future cases addressing conscience protections will no doubt rely on the standing justification in *Alliance* for delineating their scope. Through this sleight of hand, the court has transformed a case that averts a shift in reproductive rights on the basis of standing to one that accomplishes a key conservative ideological goal in the effort to limit reproductive choice.

NEXT STEPS

Nothing in this term's *Alliance* decision prevents other cases of a similar nature from being brought to challenge the FDA's authority to expand access to mifepristone, if those cases are brought by plaintiffs who can establish standing. The most likely next case will be brought by the three states that unsuccessfully sought to intervene in the *Alliance* case itself, but only late in the proceedings when the question of standing first loomed as a threat to the success of the original claimants' case.[23] These states will argue in future litigation that they experience direct harm from adverse patient outcomes attributable to the FDA's decisions, in the form of subsidized medical care and mental health care.[24]

That these state claims of standing are likely to be successful (without regard to the merits) is presaged by the Court's recent decision in *Biden v. Nebraska*. In that 2023 case, the Court held that Missouri had standing to challenge the Biden Administration's student loan forgiveness plan.[25] The basis of Missouri's claim to standing was through its relationship to the Missouri Higher Education Loan Authority (MOHELA) an independent public corporation charged with holding and servicing student loans and collecting fees on behalf of the state.[26] The Court found that a reduction

---

[23] See Notice of Intervention Below, and Motion of Missouri, Idaho, and Kansas to Intervene in FDA v. All. for Hippocratic Med; motion to intervene den'd, *Danco Lab'ys, L.L.C. v. All. for Hippocratice Med.*, 2024 U.S.Lexis 699.

[24] See Notice of Intervention Below, and Motion of Missouri, Idaho, and Kansas to Intervene in FDA v. All. for Hippocratic Med. at 8.

[25] *Biden v. Nebraska*, 600 U.S. 477, 483, 494 (2023).

[26] *Id.* at 490, 492.

in the administrative fees MOHELA was able to collect was a "financial harm" to Missouri "directly traceable to the Secretary's plan."[27] If Missouri was successful in establishing standing because of the impact of student loans on MOHELA, it and other states are likely to be able to do so regarding the impact of alleged adverse consequences of mifepristone on state-financed medical care.

As an antidote to the lack of standing, the *Alliance* majority suggests as well that citizens with "sincere concerns about ... others using mifepristone" may "take their concerns to the Executive and Legislative Branches."[28] A new administration friendly to the perspective of the plaintiffs may instead advance the goals of this litigation by either prevailing upon the FDA to reverse its approvals[29] or by reanimating the nineteenth-century Comstock Law to prohibit the use of mail or other delivery services for these or similar medications.[30] Whether through renewed litigation with stronger standing claims or by executive action, the threat to continued availability of medical abortion will no doubt return to the federal courts in the coming years.

---

[27] *Id.*

[28] *Alliance*, 602 U.S. at 369.

[29] See Project 2025: Mandate for Leadership: The Conservative Promise at 459 (urging the FDA's reversal of mifepristone approval).

[30] See *Id.* at 562 (referencing 18 U.S. Code §§ 1461 and 1462).

CHAPTER 5

Moyle v. U.S.: Court Restores Injunction Against Idaho Abortion Ban; Decision on the Merits Postponed

Leslie F. Goldstein

On June 27, the Supreme Court handed down a *per curiam* (unsigned) decision for the cases *Moyle v. U.S.S.* and *Idaho v. U.S.S.*[1] with an order that sounds less consequential than it is: "The writs of certiorari before judgment are dismissed as improvidently granted, and the stays entered by the Court on January 5, 2024, are vacated."

---

[1] Officially two separate cases, they basically present the same issues. One petitioner is the State of Idaho and the other is the Speaker of the Idaho House of Representatives.

Historic Background

The background of the decision is as follows: *Griswold v. Connecticut*,[2] *Eisenstadt v. Baird*,[3] *Roe v. Wade*,[4] and *Planned Parenthood v. Casey*,[5] all presented the constitutional right of reproductive privacy as a right protected as a fundamental aspect of the liberty enshrined in the Fourteenth and Fifth Amendment due process clauses. The reproductive privacy acknowledged in these precedents included the right to obtain, with a licensed doctor's approval, an abortion of any previable fetus. As to an already viable fetus, the Court ruled that preserving its life was a compelling enough societal interest that states might ban terminating the pregnancy *unless the pregnancy threatened the "life or health" of the pregnant woman* (my emphasis).

Then in 2022 the *Dobbs v. Jackson WHO* decision singled out out *Roe v. Wade* (and its follow-up *Planned Parenthood v. Casey*) not as having been about reproductive freedom but simply about "the right to obtain an abortion," and declared that there is no such constitutional right. *Dobbs* opened the floodgates to a spate of state-level bans on abortion.[6] One such state was Idaho.

Idaho Chronology

On August 24, 2022, a Federal District Court issued an injunction, pending litigation, that blocked a 2020 Idaho statute ("Total Abortion Ban"), which contained a "trigger provision" stating that the law would

---

[2] 381 U.S. 479 (1965), establishing a constitutional right to marital privacy in the decision whether use and purchase contraceptives.

[3] 405 U.S. 438 (1972), establishing the broader right to reproductive privacy as "the right of an individual, married or single, to be free from unwarranted government intrusion into… the decision *whether to bear* or beget *a child*". My emphasis.

[4] 410 U.S. 113, establishing a constitutional right to obtain an abortion.

[5] 505 U.S. 833 (1991), modifying the trimester framework of *Roe* in favor of treating the point of viability as the dividing line. Prior to fetal viability states could regulate the practice of abortion, so long as the regulation did not "undu[ly] burden" the woman's exercise of her right to reproductive freedom. Even after the point of viability, if the pregnancy threatened a woman's life or health, (as in *Roe v. Wade*) her own right to self-preservation allowed her to let a doctor to terminate even a viable fetus. *Id.*, at 860, 870.

[6] *Dobbs v. Jackson Women's Health Organization*, 597 U.S. 215 (2022).

take effect immediately upon the overturning of *Roe v. Wade*.[7] The Total Abortion Ban rendered the performing or attempting to perform an abortion at any point after fertilization a felony carrying a 2–5 year prison sentence.[8] The Court reasoned that the Idaho statute directly clashed with the Federal Emergency Medical Treatment and Labor Act (EMTALA). In the District Court's words, the "EMTALA requires that ER physicians at hospitals receiving Medicare funds offer stabilizing treatment to patients who arrive with emergency medical conditions. But when the stabilizing treatment is an abortion, offering that care is a crime under Idaho Code § 18–622—which, in its terms, bans all abortions." The judge detailed the situation:

> if the physician does not perform the abortion, the pregnant patient faces grave risks to her health—such as severe sepsis requiring limb amputation, uncontrollable uterine hemorrhage requiring hysterectomy, kidney failure requiring lifelong dialysis, hypoxic brain injury, or even [eventual] death. And this woman, if she lives, potentially may have to live the remainder of her life with significant disabilities and chronic medical conditions as a result of her pregnancy complication....[9]

Since the EMTALA required performing the abortion if needed to prevent serious harm, the state's criminalization of such abortions appeared to clash directly with federal law and thus likely to be found unconstitutional under the Supremacy Clause of the Constitution (Art VI, Clause 2).

In 2023 the Idaho Supreme Court heard a challenge to the Total Abortion Ban brought under the Idaho Constitution. The court ruled that the law did not conflict with the state's constitution, but it also interpreted the ban to "not require objective certainty, or a particular level of immediacy, before the abortion can be 'necessary' to save the woman's life," and ruled that removing any not medically viable pregnancy would not count as "abortion" in Idaho.[10] In response, the Idaho

---

[7] Idaho Code § 18–622.

[8] *U.S. v. State of Idaho*, 623 F. Supp. 3d 1096, 1111 (2022).

[9] *Id.*, at 1101.

[10] Planned Parenthood Great Nw. v. State, 171 Idaho 374, 445, 522 P. 3d 1132, 1203 (2023).

legislature amended the Total Abortion Ban, to incorporate the exemptions for terminating the pregnancy to remove "a dead unborn child," an ectopic fetus, or a molar pregnancy and clarified standards of liability so that doctors need not fear having to defend against a prosecution, for instance, for terminating a pregnancy to prevent the likely (albeit neither certain nor immediately pending) death of the pregnant woman.[11]

On Sep 28, 2023, a panel of three Trump-appointed judges on the Ninth Circuit Court of Appeals lifted the injunction that blocked the Total Abortion Ban pending litigation, but then on October 10, 2023, the whole Ninth Circuit *en banc* reinstated the injunction, blocking Idaho from enforcing the abortion ban in medical emergencies during the litigation and setting a date for oral arguments on the law's constitutionality.[12] At this point, on January 5, 2024, the U.S. Supreme Court intervened, staying the District Court injunction and granting cert to hear the case itself prior to the Circuit's judgment.

Now, with permission from the U.S. Supreme Court, Idaho began enforcing its Total Abortion Ban. As a consequence, Idaho's largest provider of emergency medical services (for instance) had to airlift a pregnant woman for urgent medical care to another state, on average, once every two weeks. The average frequency for such flights in years prior to the Ban had been once a year.[13] Naturally, such a procedure would have enhanced the risk of harm for a woman already in a medical emergency situation.

THE U.S. SUPREME COURT OPINIONS

After six months of this state of the law, the U.S. Supreme Court finally changed its mind and lifted the stay on the injunction, reinstating the judicial blocking the Total Abortion Ban. The court divided 6–3 on lifting

---

[11] I.C. §18–604(1)(b), (c); §18– 622(2).

[12] National Women's Health Center, "Idaho v. United States and Moyle v. United States: The Supreme Court Will Decide If States Can Block Pregnant People from Getting Emergency Abortion Care, February 16, 2024." https://nwlc.org/resource/idaho-v-united-states-and-moyle-v-united-states-the-supreme-court-will-decide-if-states-can-block-pregnant-people-from-getting-emergency-abortion-care/ accessed July 27. 2024.

[13] Moyle v. U.S., of JUSTICE KAGAN, with whom JUSTICE SOTOMAYOR joins, and with whom JUSTICE JACKSON joins as to Part II, concurring, slip opinion p. 2.

the stay and dismissing the early grant of review of the underlying issues; the justices would hear the main case only after the Circuit Court of Appeals had a chance to hear the arguments on the merits and issue a ruling, the normal course of events.

While the ruling was officially *per curiam* (by the Court as a whole), the reasoning that the justices provided for ruling revealed the Court to be deeply fragmented over the questions presented.

In dissent, Alito, Thomas, and Jackson all wanted to decide immediately the basic question of whether the State law conflicted with the federal law and was therefore unconstitutional, but they wanted the Court to reach opposite conclusions. Jackson insisted the women's need for medical emergency care meant that the Ban needed to be struck down immediately. Alito, with Thomas (and with Gorsuch on this point), argued that the state law was compatible with the federal law and therefore not unconstitutional. Their basic reason was that the EMTALA mandated that emergency medical providers seek to preserve the life of the fetus. Justices Jackson, Sotomayor, and Kagan understood this preservation mandate to apply only to those situations where the fetus *itself* needed emergency care, not to situations where the pregnancy threatened the woman's life or health.

The second reason that Alito and Thomas identified for immediately upholding the Idaho law was that they questioned the constitutionality of the provisions in the EMTALA requiring emergency abortions in Medicare recipient hospitals. There is a wide-ranging array of precedents on when Congress is and is not allowed to attach restrictions on entities that receive federal funds. Alito and Thomas concluded that these precedents rendered the EMTALA unconstitutional. Justice Jackson again disagreed with them.

Thus, even though the Court majority preferred to formally postpone its decision as to the constitutionality of the state law, several justices set forth their views on the constitutionality question. The Court divided 3–3 on the probable or certain finding of unconstitutionality of the state law question: Kagan with Sotomayor (probable) and Jackson (certain); and in favor of constitutionality, Alito with Thomas (certain) and Gorsuch (probable).

The other three justices, in an opinion by Justice Barrett, joined by Justice Kavanaugh and Chief Justice Roberts, reasoned that so many legal changes had transpired between the initial grant of *certiorari* and stay of the injunction that it was now at least in principle possible to rule that the two laws no longer clashed to any significant degree. Moreover, the issue of whether the federal government acted beyond its powers in mandating certain hospital actions that would violate state law as a condition on the receipt of federal funds was new. The vote of these three, plus Gorsuch, Sotomayor, and Kagan, comprised the group of justices who dismissed the grant of *certiorari* and lifted the stay to reinstate the Total Abortion Ban from being enforced until the final judicial resolution of the issues.

In addition, Barrett's opinion noted important legal changes that had come about in the briefs of both sides. (1) The US. would not interpret the EMTALA to cover mental health concerns for emergency treatment; (2) the U.S. would allow individual doctors with conscientious scruples against doing abortions to opt out. (3) Idaho attorneys added to the already-itemized exemptions from prosecutable abortions most of the additional causes for emergency abortions: eclampsia, pre-eclampsia, PPROM, placental abruption, heart failure, and sepsis.[14] Since both parties' "positions were still evolving," Justice Barrett and her two colleagues maintained that it made sense to let the issues be fleshed out further in the Court of Appeals, before the Supreme Court needed to decide whether to intervene.

Conclusion

A. The Law

The pregnant women of Idaho needing emergency medical care have received a reprieve against state's Total Abortion Ban. This reprieve will last for perhaps a year or two, however long it takes for the Appeals Court to decide the pre-emption case and for the U.S. Supreme Court to decide whether to grant *certiorari* again and to decide whether or not to uphold whatever conclusion is reached by the Circuit Court decision.

B. The Puzzle with a Suggested Resolution

Three justices, if deciding solely on the merits would have ruled the Idaho statute invalid as pre-empted (Sotomayor, Kagan, and Jackson), since it directly conflicts with a federal law. Three would have ruled it

---

[14] Barrett, slip opinion 5–6.

constitutional (Thomas, Alito, and Gorsuch), seeing no conflict between the two laws because they believed the EMTLA *itself*, like the Idaho law, forbids medical emergency abortions, and they argued that Congress is not constitutionally allowed to use its spending power to compel hospitals to violate state laws. Three others reject this reading of the EMTALA as forbidding medical emergency abortions and believe that at the current time, there may be no conflict between the Idaho state law and the federal law, but these final three also consider unresolved the question of whether the spending power of Congress allows it to restrict state behavior in this way.

If the first threesome prevailed, *all* the states that have laws similar to the Idaho ban would lose their prohibitions on medical emergency abortions (or have to give up federal funding). If the second three prevailed, medically necessary but *not* life-threatening abortions would be *forbidden* by federal law (for hospitals with federal funding) all over the U.S. If the middle three (the third group) were to prevail on the merits, the Idaho case would be dropped as moot, because there would no longer be a need for federal intervention. The EMTALA would still be read as requiring medically necessary emergency abortions, but a suit would need to be brought from another state in order to get rid of the laws of states other than Idaho that conflict with this EMTALA provision. There would be no effective ruling here.

What persuaded Gorsuch, Sotomayor, and Kagan to be willing to postpone a decision on constitutionality for their respective favored result and instead to join the per curiam (instead of dissenting on the merits, for now)? Their decisions gave the Court a majority, so that the outcome was not a confusing 3-3-3.

To Sotomayor and Kagan, Barrett's decision offered the olive branch of lifting the injunction right away, so that the Total Abortion Ban of Idaho was now again blocked from endangering women's lives (and the Supreme Court was implying that similar injunctions might be issued elsewhere). And the incentive that Barrett offered to Gorsuch for accepting postponement may have been her throwing into her three-justice opinion this sentence: "On top of that, petitioners have raised a difficult and consequential argument, which they did not discuss in their stay applications, about whether Congress, in reliance on the Spending Clause, can obligate recipients of federal funds to violate state criminal law." Now Gorsuch could hope that the lower court would flesh out the arguments against allowing Congress in the EMTALA to restrict hospital behavior in the way it seemed to be doing, thereby allowing the kind of state restriction on abortion that Idaho had attempted. So he, too, had reason to join the *per curiam*.

What will become of this 3-3-3 division on the case's second visit to the Supreme Court remains to be seen.

CHAPTER 6

Consumer Finance Protection Bureau v. Community Financial Services Ass'n: When Is an Appropriation Not an Appropriation?

Chase Porter

When is an appropriation not an appropriation? This is the conundrum that the Supreme Court faced in *Consumer Financial Protection Bureau v. Community Financial Services Association of America, Limited*. The CFPB was formed in 2011 by the Dodd-Frank Act.[1] The Bureau states that it "implements and enforces Federal consumer financial law and ensures that markets for consumer financial products are fair, transparent,

---

[1] Dodd-Frank Wall Street Reform and Consumer Protection Act, Pub. L. No. 111–203, § 1011, 124 Stat. 1376, 1964 (2010) (codified at 12 U.S.C. § 5491). The stated purpose of the Dodd-Frank Act is "to promote the financial stability of the United States by improving accountability and transparency in the financial system, to end 'too big to fail', to protect the American taxpayer by ending bailouts, to protect consumers from abusive financial services practices, and for other purposes." (Pub. L. No, 111–203, 124 Stat. 1376, 1376). While the law was passed in 2010, the CFPB did not begin functioning until 2011.

C. Porter (✉)
California Baptist University, Riverside, CA, USA
e-mail: cporter@calbaptist.edu

© The Author(s), under exclusive license to Springer Nature Switzerland AG 2025
H. Schweber (ed.), *SCOTUS 2024*,
https://doi.org/10.1007/978-3-031-78551-1_6

and competitive."[2] It is an independent agency with two structural features that have raised constitutional questions before the Supreme Court. In *Seila Law LLC v. CFPB*,[3] the Court determined that the presidential appointment of an agency director who could then only be removed for causes specified by Congress violated the separation of powers, but also held that the CFPB could continue to exist if that defect was remedied. *CFPB v. CFSAA* involved a challenge to the way the CFPB is funded. And it started because of another controversial source of funding: payday loans.

In 2017, the CFPB proposed 12 CFR Part 1041, known as the Payday Lending Rule. The original version took effect in 2018, and after various court challenges and amendments, the final version took effect on October 20, 2020. In Section 1041.8(b), the CFPB placed a limit on the number of times that a payday lender could attempt to automatically withdraw a loan payment from a consumer's bank account. Payday lenders were banned from attempting a third automatic transfer if two consecutive transfers had failed unless they had received consent from the consumer to initiate another withdrawal. The regulation was designed to prevent consumers from accumulating bank fees for failed withdrawals. Since the regulation limited the ability of payday lenders to collect loan repayments, CFSAA, the trade organization that represents some payday lenders, asked the federal courts to void the regulation on three separate grounds. The CFSAA challenged the authority of the CFPB director to issue the regulation due to its original issuance under an unconstitutional structure (per *Seila Law*) and alleged that proper rulemaking procedures had not been followed. While the Fifth Circuit rejected both arguments, it was the third argument that was accepted which made its way to the Supreme Court. Rather than simply challenging the specific regulation, the CFSAA also questioned the very right of the CFPB to exist due to a unique funding mechanism. The Fifth Circuit accepted the argument that the funding mechanism was a violation of the Appropriations Clause, and the federal government appealed to the Supreme Court.[4]

---

[2] Consumer Financial Protection Bureau, *About Us*, https://www.consumerfinance.gov/about-us/.

[3] *Seila Law LLC v. Consumer Financial Protection Bureau*, 591 U.S. 197 (2020).

[4] *Community Financial Services Association of America v. Consumer Financial Protection Bureau*, 51 F. 4th 616 (5th Cir. 2022).

The Appropriations Clause (Article I, Section 9, Clause 7), states that "No Money shall be drawn from the Treasury, but in Consequence of Appropriations made by Law." In other words, for the government to spend money, Congress must pass a law authorizing the expenditure. When Congress established the CFPB, Congress developed a funding mechanism that is doubly insulated from the traditional appropriations process to preserve the agency's independence. Rather than Congress providing the CFPB with an annual budget, the CFPB is allowed to request an annual budget from the Federal Reserve, up to a certain inflation-adjusted percentage of the Federal Reserve's budget. However, the Federal Reserve itself is also not funded via an annual appropriation from Congress; instead, it is funded through fees that it charges. The Fifth Circuit agreed that this doubly insulated funding mechanism unconstitutionally removed the funding of the CFPB from the control of Congress and therefore violated the Appropriations Clause. Thus, the Supreme Court was faced with an interesting question: when is an appropriation not an appropriation?

Essentially, the argument revolved around the elements required for a grant of funding to be considered a constitutional appropriation, and if one of those elements is a requirement for an appropriation to be renewed by Congress on a regular basis. The Clause itself provides no guidance beyond the requirement that an appropriation be made by law. There is a second part of the Clause (the Statement and Account Clause) that requires the publication of "receipts and expenditures" from "time to time," but there is no similar language that applies to the first half of the Clause.

In a 7–2 decision authored by Justice Thomas, the majority held that there are only two elements required for constitutionality. "Appropriations need only identify a source of public funds and authorize the expenditure of those funds for designated purposes."[5] Congress satisfied these two elements with the funding mechanism for CFPB. The source of funding is the Federal Reserve, and the designated purposes for the funding are to accomplish the purposes of the CFPB as defined in the enabling legislation. To define the word "appropriation," Justice Thomas adopted an original public meaning approach and surveyed both contemporary dictionaries and how various legislatures approached

---

[5] *Consumer Financial Protection Bureau et. al. v. Community Financial Services Association of America, Ltd., et. al.*, 601 US ___ (2024), No. 22–448, slip op. at 6.

appropriations at the time of the ratification of the Constitution to distill the minimum required elements for an appropriation. Additionally, he considered the history of England, particularly the changes in the financial relationship between the monarchy and Parliament that were brought about by the Glorious Revolution of 1688. Pre-Revolution, the monarchy's funding "inhered in the king himself" and thus "Parliament had little claim to direct how it was spent."[6] Post-Revolution, the monarchy became more dependent on Parliament for sources of funding, which consequently gave Parliament more ability to define how revenue would be spent. But Thomas observed that "even with this newfound fiscal supremacy, Parliament did not micromanage every aspect of the King's finances. Not all post-Glorious Revolution grants of supplies were time limited."[7] In other words, while Parliament started to set limits on how money could be spent, it did not always provide limits to how long that money could be spent without seeking reauthorization.

"The appropriations practice in the Colonies and early state legislatures was much the same."[8] Thomas cited several examples of what he called "open-ended, discretionary appropriations."[9] The legislative branch defined a general purpose for the appropriation, but then granted the discretionary right to other branches and agencies to determine the specifics of how and on what timetable the appropriation would be spent. This understanding of appropriations was apparently so well-established by the time of the Constitutional Convention that the only debate involving the Clause was over which chamber of Congress should originate appropriations legislation. Congress followed the "source-and-purpose approach" after the ratification of the Constitution. This even included permitting funding schemes that depended on revenue collected by agencies themselves, such as customs collectors and the Post Office.[10]

In addition to the original public meaning argument, the majority affirmed two arguments rooted in the structure of the Constitution. The Appropriations Clause is found in Article I, Section 9, among a list of limitations on the powers of Congress. It is not found in Article I, Section 8,

---

[6] *Id.*, slip op. at 8.
[7] *Id.*, slip op. at 9.
[8] *Id.*, slip op. at 10.
[9] *Id.*, slip op. at 10.
[10] *Id.*, slip op. at 14.

which affirmatively lists the enumerated and elastic powers of Congress. Thus, Thomas argued that rather than granting the power of appropriations to Congress, the Constitution assumes that Congress possesses the power and then places textual limits on the exercise of that power. One limit in the Appropriations Clause is that there can be no appropriation without a law. A second limit is found in the enumerated powers of Congress. While Congress has the power to fund a military, appropriations for an Army (as opposed to a Navy) are time-limited to two years (Article I, Section 8, Clause 12). Since the Constitution time-limits military appropriations but no other types, the majority contended that there is, in fact, an assumed appropriations power that is not time-limited unless specifically limited by the text. Thus, the Court rejected the three arguments put forward by the CFSAA: the "source" of the appropriations does not have to be Congress itself, the appropriation does not have to be time-limited, and the funding scheme does not violate the separation of powers structure of Article I.

Two justices joined the majority's opinion in full but wrote separate concurrences. In Justice Kagan's concurrence (joined by Justice Sotomayor, Kavanaugh, and Barrett), she stressed that the original public meaning of appropriation discerned by the majority continues to be the meaning today. As she noted, "the founding-era practice that the Court relates became the 19th-century practice, which became the 20th-century practice, which became today's. For over 200 years now, Congress has exercised broad discretion in crafting appropriations."[11] In fact, the continuing tradition of discretionary appropriations without time limits is now so prevalent that in FY2022, two-thirds of the federal budget did not require periodic appropriations.[12] Justice Jackson separately concurred to note that the wisdom of the funding mechanism is a political question for Congress to resolve. In her view, the majority correctly discerned a source-and-purpose understanding of the term "appropriation" and correctly determined that Congress had designated a source and a purpose for the CFPB appropriation. Thus, no further analysis is needed. The Constitution does not designate any limits to the appropriations power

---

[11] *Id.*, slip op. at 2 (Kagan, J.).
[12] *Id.*, slip op. at 3 (Kagan, J.)

that would apply in this case; thus, the Court "should not lightly assume that Article III implicitly directs the Judiciary to find one."[13]

Justices Alito and Gorsuch dissented from the majority's understanding of the Appropriations Clause, arguing that the interpretation turns the Clause into a "minor vestige." Alito interestingly observed that Congress itself tried to preempt Appropriations Clause challenges to the funding structure both by explicitly stating that the funding should not be considered an appropriation and that the funding was not subject to the oversight of the Committees on Appropriations.[14] Alito noted that during oral arguments, the government conceded that the majority's interpretation would allow for a government agency to be funded by purely private sources. Additionally, using a citation from Montesquieu's *The Spirit of the Law*, Alito contended that appropriations without a time limit will cause the legislature to "lose its power of the purse."[15] These considerations are pragmatic ones, by which the dissenters considered the practical consequences of the separation of powers structure.

However, the bulk of Alito's dissent was dedicated to a historical analysis of the term "appropriation," but through a lens that differed from the majority. Alito rejected the original public meaning approach of Thomas, arguing that the public meaning is not a relevant consideration when dealing with a term of the art such as "appropriation." Put differently, since the word is a legal term, the proper interpretation of the term must occur using the legal background which informed the term, rather than the contemporary usage at the time of ratification. Ultimately, Alito's approach becomes a distinction without a difference, as he resorted to much of the same historical interpretation that Thomas did in the majority opinion. While Alito claimed that his interpretive methodology differs from Thomas' due to his focus on the technical legal meaning of appropriation, he acknowledged that the majority examined the same history of terms that he did. They just arrived at different conclusions. For instance, Alito cited evidence from post-Glorious Revolution England about the usual appropriation practices of Parliament, such as initiating an expectation of the need for the annual justification of appropriations to the

---

[13] *Id.*, slip op. at 1 (Jackson, J.).

[14] *Id.*, slip op. at 4–5 (Alito, J.).

[15] *Id.*, slip op. at 2 (Alito, J.).

monarchy.[16] Interestingly, Alito's evidence about the annual justification requirement was drawn from the majority opinion. As another example, when speaking of the American practice, Alito noted this: "Although the Constitution does not require that appropriations be limited to a single year, that was the dominant practice in the years immediately following the adoption of the Constitution."[17] The "dominant practice" language is key for understanding the difference in how the majority and dissent read history. For the dissent, a practice being "dominant" is dispositive. For the majority, examples of appropriations that are discretionary or not time-limited provide dispositive evidence that the legislative branch was willing to make those types of appropriations. For his part, Thomas argued that the different conclusions arose because Alito ignored relevant parts of the historical record.[18] What Alito originally framed as a debate over appropriate interpretive methodology ultimately morphed into a disagreement over the significance of various pieces of historical evidence.

Thomas critiqued Alito's historical interpretation on the grounds that the analysis did not lead to an understanding of what the term "appropriations" means. But the strict meaning of the term was not Alito's primary concern; instead, Alito was focused on the separation of powers consequences of adopting the majority's source-and-purpose understanding of the Appropriations Clause. In *Seila Law*, Alito and Thomas were on the same side of the separation of powers question. However, the central question in *Seila Law* was a structural issue resolved by reference to history and precedent, not a textual interpretation issue. Thus, Alito and Thomas aligned over structural concerns with the removal mechanism in *Seila Law*; here, they differed over textual interpretation. Thomas argued that any separation of powers concerns in *CFPB v. CFSAA* were ameliorated by the fact that Congress itself designed the funding system. Both justices had separation of powers in view; Thomas was just convinced that the funding mechanism met the separation of powers obligations explicitly in the text. It is not as if the CFPB was funding itself completely independently from Congress. It was simply following the system that Congress authorized.

---

[16] *Id.*, slip op. at 12 (Alito, J.).

[17] *Id.*, slip op. at 14 (Alito, J.).

[18] *Id.*, slip op. at 19–22.

By contrast, Alito's dissent hinged on his overall disapproval of the design of the CFPB as an institution. He dismissed the Post Office and Customs Service analogies on the basis that those agencies possess narrowly defined missions, whereas the CFPB's powers are "broad and vast."[19] He argued that the funding system is a unique combination of features that creates a novel scheme among government agencies that was "carefully designed to give the Bureau maximum unaccountability."[20] Rather than a technical concern with when an appropriation is, in fact, an appropriation, Alito saw the Appropriations Clause as a tool for agency accountability that in his view was not being properly used in this case.

Who has the history correct? Christine Chabot points to further historical examples of early appropriations that did not have time limitations.[21] However, the historical debate arguably loses some relevance when one realizes that the original public meaning approach of Thomas and the structural analysis approach of Alito are like two ships passing in the night. Thomas focused on the meaning of a word; Alito focused on the structural consequences of that meaning. Perhaps it is significant that the only justice to join in Alito's dissent was Gorsuch, who is well-known for his anti-agency jurisprudence.[22] The bureaucracy was dealt a significant blow this term with the overturning of the *Chevron* doctrine. But for now, the CFPB lives to regulate another day, and the payday loan repayment rule stands.

---

[19] *Id.*, slip op. at 19–20 (Alito, J.).

[20] *Id.*, Slip op. at 21 (Alito, J.).

[21] Christine Kexel Chabot, "The Founders' Purse." 110 VIRG. L. REV. 5 (2024).

[22] For an excellent example of Justice Gorsuch's thoughts on the administrative state, see his concurrence in *Loper Bright Enterprises v. Raimondo*, 603 US ___ (2024), No. 22-451, slip op. (Gorsuch, J.). See also Gillian E. Metzger, "1930s Redux: The Administrative State under Siege," 131 HARV. L. REV. 1 (2017). Metzger analyzes anti-administrative state positions that Gorsuch took prior to his appointment to the Supreme Court.

CHAPTER 7

Securities and Exchange Commission v. Jarkesy: New Limits on Administrative Adjudication

William Funk

Background

The securities statutes passed in response to the 1929 stock market crash include antifraud provisions to be enforced by the Securities and Exchange Commission (SEC). Originally, the SEC could only seek civil penalties in federal court, but in 2010 Congress amended the law to enable the SEC to obtain civil penalties in administrative proceedings as well.

In 2013, the SEC initiated an administrative enforcement action against George Jarkesy, seeking civil penalties for securities fraud. The Administrative Law Judge (ALJ) found Jarkesy liable and issued a cease-and-desist order and a $300,000 civil penalty. Jarkesy appealed this decision to the whole Commission, which affirmed the ALJ's decision. Jarkesy then sought judicial review. Rather than challenge the actual SEC

W. Funk (✉)
Lewis and Clark University, Portland, Oregon, USA
e-mail: funk@lclark.edu

© The Author(s), under exclusive license to Springer Nature Switzerland AG 2025
H. Schweber (ed.), *SCOTUS 2024*,
https://doi.org/10.1007/978-3-031-78551-1_7

decision, Jarkesy challenged the constitutionality of the system by which the decision had been made. Specifically, he claimed that issuing a civil penalty administratively violated the Seventh Amendment to the Constitution, which provides a right to a jury trial in "suits at common law."[1] In addition, he argued that providing the SEC the option of proceeding administratively or judicially, without any guidance to the SEC as to when it should proceed one way or the other, was an unconstitutional delegation of legislative power.[2] Finally, he claimed that the insulation of the ALJ from removal by imposing dual for-cause removal requirements violated the separation of powers.[3] A divided panel of the Fifth Circuit agreed with each of these claims,[4] and the Supreme Court granted certiorari upon the SEC's petition.

The Opinion

The Supreme Court by a 6–3 margin affirmed the Fifth Circuit's decision with respect to the Seventh Amendment claim and did not address the other two constitutional issues.[5] The Chief Justice, joined by Justices Thomas, Alito, Kavanaugh, Gorsuch, and Barrett, began by asking whether a case alleging fraud was akin to "suits at common law." Because federal law long ago eliminated the distinction between suits "at law" and suits "in equity,"[6] the Court has long held that courts must ask whether

---

[1] U.S. Const., 7th Amendment.

[2] The Supreme Court has said that Congress may not delegate its legislative powers to executive agencies unless it provides an intelligible principle to guide the exercise of that delegation. *See, e.g., Gundy v. United States*, 588 U.S. 128 (2019).

[3] An SEC ALJ may only be removed for cause upon a complaint by the SEC, whose members arguably may only be removed for cause, and a determination of cause by the Merit Systems Protection Board, whose members may only be removed for cause. In *Free Enterprise Fund v. Public Co. Accounting Oversight Board*, 561 U.S. 477 (2010), the Supreme Court held that a dual for-cause removal protection for members of the Public Company Accounting Oversight Board unconstitutionally insulated them from Presidential oversight.

[4] *Jarkesy v. Securities and Exchange Comm'n*, 34 F.4th 446 (5th Cir. 2022).

[5] *Securities and Exchange Comm'n v. Jarkesy*, 144 S.Ct. 2117 (2024).

[6] At the time of the founding, as had long been the case in England, courts were either common law courts or courts of equity. Common law courts employed juries as fact-finders and courts of equity, derived from Chancery Courts in England, did not. Common law courts generally provided damages as a remedy for a winning plaintiff.

the suit in question, even under a new statute, would have been a suit at law historically or is akin to such a suit, in which case the Seventh Amendment would apply. Here, the Court said, two factors indicated that the SEC's fraud enforcement was akin to suit at law. First and foremost, "the remedy is all but dispositive."[7] Civil penalties are a form of monetary relief, and "money damages are the prototypical common law remedy."[8] Moreover, monetary impositions designed to punish and deter, rather than compensate, were "a type of remedy at common law that could only be enforced in courts of law."[9] Consequently, the SEC's civil penalty actions were sufficiently similar to historical examples of suits at common law that they were subject to the Seventh Amendment's requirements.

In addition, the Court said, the close relationship between the causes of action in an SEC fraud case and common law fraud confirmed the conclusion that this was akin to a suit at common law, thereby requiring the right to a jury trial. By using the common law term "fraud" in the statute, Congress "incorporated prohibitions from common law fraud into federal securities law."[10] The Court acknowledged that the statutory securities fraud was not identical with common law fraud in some significant respects. First, statutory securities fraud only targeted certain subject matter and disclosures rather than the broader range of common law fraud that might be related to a securities violation. Second, federal securities fraud only requires proof beyond by a preponderance of the evidence, whereas common law fraud typically used a more stringent standard. Third, unlike common law fraud, federal securities fraud does not require a showing of harm. "Nevertheless, the close relationship between federal securities fraud and common law fraud confirms that this action is 'legal in nature.'".[11]

Nevertheless, the Court had to deal with the so-called "public rights" exception to the general requirement that cases must be heard in an

---

Courts of equity, on the other hand, typically issued an order to the losing defendant to do or refrain from doing something, what we call an injunction. In the mid-twentieth century, federal law eliminated the two different courts, merging them into one court, which exercises both forms of judicial power.

[7] *Ibid.*, at 2129.

[8] *Ibid.*

[9] *Ibid.*, (quoting *Tull v. United States*, 481 U.S. 412, 422 (1987).

[10] *Ibid.*, at 2130.

[11] *Ibid.*

Article III court at all. Because if a case need not be heard in a court but instead before an administrative tribunal, then the Seventh Amendment would not apply. "Public rights" cases "historically could have been determined exclusively by [the executive and legislative] branches."[12] The general requirement for a case to be heard in an Article III court applies to cases involving "private rights."

Since the earliest days of the Republic, Congress has with the approval of the Supreme Court assigned certain types of cases to non-Article III courts. In 1856, the Court upheld the executive determinations of collections of revenue[13]; in 1899, it upheld administrative adjudications of patent rights[14]; in 1909, it upheld the administrative imposition of a monetary penalty for violations of immigration laws[15]; in 1929, the Court upheld the ability of the executive to impose tariffs as a penalty for importing goods by unfair methods of competition[16]; in 1932, it upheld the administrative adjudication of cases involving the administration of public lands, the granting of public benefits and pensions[17]; and in 1977, the Court approved the administrative imposition of civil penalties for violations of the Occupational Health and Safety Administration's regulations.[18] As the Court said in 1932, "[f]amiliar illustrations of administrative agencies created for the determination of [public rights] matters are found in connection with the exercise of the congressional power as to interstate and foreign commerce, taxation, immigration, the public lands, public health, the facilities of the post office, pensions, and payments to veterans."[19] And then, of course, there are the "courts" of the territories and District of Columbia as well as bankruptcy courts, none of which are Article III courts.

---

[12] *Ibid.*, at 2132 (quoting *Murray's Lessee v. Hoboken Land & Improvement Co.*, 18 How. 272, 493 (1856).

[13] See *Murray's Lessee v. Hoboken Land & Improvement Co.*, 18 How. 272 (1856).

[14] See *United States v. Duell*, 172 U.S. 576 (1899).

[15] See *Oceanic Steam Navigation Co. v. Stranahan*, 214 U.S. 320 (1909).

[16] See *Ex parte Bakelite Corp.*, 279 US. 438 (1929).

[17] See *Crowell v. Benson*, 285 U.S. 22 (1932).

[18] See *Atlas Roofing Co. v. Occupational Safety and Health Review Commission*, 430 U.S. 442 (1977).

[19] *Crowell v. Benson, supra*, at 50.

Notwithstanding this history, the Court found that Congress's grant of power to the SEC to assess civil penalties administratively was unconstitutional, because it did not fit within these historical exceptions. The Court stated that each of these exceptions derived from the fact that the particular authority being exercised was in some way special—the exclusive or plenary authority of Congress over foreign commerce, taxation, immigration, and the public lands, for example. However, Congress's authority to police fraud in securities trading apparently was different and did not qualify for an exception.

The nearest case in point was *Atlas Roofing*,[20] which involved a civil penalty imposed administratively by the Occupational Safety and Health Administration (OSHA). There the Supreme Court unanimously[21] upheld the penalty against a Seventh Amendment claim. The *Jarkesy* Court distinguished *Atlas Roofing* on the ground that the claims there under the Occupational Safety and Health Act were unknown to the common law, whereas here the claims were in the nature of a common law suit. Nevertheless, the Court went out of its way to cast aspersions on the holding in *Atlas Roofing*, describing it as "a departure from our legal traditions."[22] In addition to quoting at length from scholarly articles that criticized *Atlas Roofing*,[23] the Court suggested that later cases had cast doubt on the analysis in *Atlas Roofing*. Consequently, the Court affirmed the Fifth Circuit's ruling on the Seventh Amendment ground.

The Concurrence

Justice Gorsuch, joined by Justice Thomas, concurred but wrote to indicate that he would go much further. In his view, the outcome in *Jarkesy* was required not just by the Seventh Amendment but also independently by Article III and the Due Process Clause. He suggested that administrative proceedings like those brought by the SEC were akin to what British colonial administrators forced upon the American colonists, and these abuses played a role in the calls for revolution. Indeed, the Declaration

---

[20] Note 18, *supra*.

[21] Unanimous among the eight justices involved in the decision. Justice Blackmun took no part in the case.

[22] *Jarkesy*, *supra*, at 2138 n. 4.

[23] *See ibid*.

of Independence called them out for abolition, and the Constitution's provision for the "judicial power" to reside in independent Article III judges was one response. Some thought greater safeguards were necessary, resulting in the Seventh Amendment's right to a jury trial in cases at common law. Finally, the Fifth Amendment's Due Process Clause declared that one may not be deprived of "life, liberty, or property" without due process of law. In Justice Gorsuch's view, the founders understood this to mean a trial in a court of law. Any exception to this must involve "some 'deeply rooted' tradition of nonjudicial adjudication."[24] Thus, the SEC's administrative adjudication of Jarkesy's violation of the securities laws was unconstitutional under each of these constitutional provisions.

The Dissent

Justice Sotomayor, joined by Justices Kagan and Jackson, dissented. Her lengthy dissent establishes that *Atlas Roofing* was neither remarkable nor novel in holding that Congress could authorize administrative agencies to impose civil penalties, subject to judicial review, for violations of federal laws and regulations. She then rebuts each of the Court's arguments for distinguishing *Atlas Roofing*. Moreover, rather than being questioned by subsequent Supreme Court cases, those cases cited *Atlas Roofing* in support of its conclusion, and Congress in reliance upon it has enacted over 200 laws providing for administrative adjudication of civil penalties.

Justice Sotomayor demonstrates that the so-called public rights "exception" has not been limited to a few special areas of federal law. Rather, it "has long been settled and undisputed that, at a minimum, a matter of public rights arises 'between the government and persons subject to its authority in connection with the performance of the constitutional functions of the executive and legislative departments.'"[25] She quotes from Justice Antonin Scalia *post Atlas Roofing*, "'from the time the doctrine of public rights was born in 1856,' everyone understood that public rights 'arise between the government and others,' and refer to '*rights of the public*—that is, rights pertaining to claims brought by or against the

---

[24] *Ibid.*, at 2147 (Gorsuch, J., concurring).

[25] *Ibid.*, at 2158–59 (quoting *Crowell v. Benson*, 285 U.S. 22, 50 (1932) (Sotomayor, J., dissenting).

United States.'"[26] In other words, when the executive enforces federal laws in the name of the public, the case involves public rights, not private rights. Thus, the SEC's case against Jarkesy involved public rights.

The majority in *Jarkesy* distinguished *Atlas Roofing* by saying that it involved claims unknown at common law. However, the Congress adopted the Occupational Safety and Health Act precisely because it found "existing state statutory remedies as well as state common-law actions for negligence and wrongful death inadequate to protect"[27] workers, just as Congress adopted the security fraud provisions in question in *Jarkesy* because it found state statutory and common-law actions for fraud inadequate to protect investors. Moreover, the Court had noted in a case after *Atlas Roofing* that "Congress may fashion causes of action that are closely analogous to common-law claims and place them beyond the ambit of the Seventh Amendment by assigning their resolution to a forum in which jury trials are unavailable. *See, e.g., Atlas Roofing* (workplace safety regulations)."[28]

Justice Sotomayor shows that the very cases which the Court used to question *Atlas Roofing* in fact cite it positively and say nothing inconsistent with its conclusion. For example, in *Granfinanciera v. Nordberg*,[29] in which the Court found that the Seventh Amendment applied to a claim in a bankruptcy proceeding, the Court distinguished *Atlas Roofing* and cited it positively. In addition, in *Tull v. United States*,[30] where the Court found that a civil penalty action which the Environmental Protection Agency had brought in federal court was subject to the Seventh Amendment, the Court again cited *Atlas Roofing* positively, noting that it involved an administrative imposition of a civil penalty, not a judicially imposed civil penalty. Only the latter involved a right to a jury trial, because juries are incompatible with administrative adjudication. No one doubted that, had the SEC proceeded judicially against Jarkesy, he would have a right to a jury trial. This highlighted how the majority in *Jarkesy* changed the way it analyzed cases involving claims of a right to a jury trial. In the

---

[26] *Ibid.*, at 2159 (quoting Scalia, J., concurring in part and concurring in the judgment, in *Granfinanciera, S. A. v. Nordberg*, 492 U.S. 33, 68–69 (1989)).

[27] *Atlas Roofing*, *supra* note 15, at 444–445.

[28] *Granfinanciera v. Nordberg*, 492 U.S. 33, 52 (1989).

[29] *Ibid.*

[30] 481 U.S. 412 (1987).

past the Court would ask first whether the case involved public rights or private rights, because if it involved public rights, the case could be administratively adjudicated rather than judicially adjudicated. Only if the case involved private rights would the Court then go on to determine whether the case was akin to a case at common law, thereby requiring a right to a jury trial. In *Jarkesy*, however, the Court first asked whether the SEC's action was akin to a case at common law, and finding that it was, then asked whether it fit within the public rights exception.

The Consequences

Strictly speaking, the Supreme Court's decision in *Jarkesy* only precludes the SEC from administratively imposing civil penalties for violation of the securities fraud statutes; the SEC retains the ability to proceed against persons in federal court for civil penalties, subject to the defendant's right to a jury trial. Moreover, the Court's opinion leaves open the ability for the SEC to seek cease-and-desist orders administratively, because those actions would be akin to cases in equity rather than the common law.

However, the Court's opinion would seem necessarily to apply to other agencies' administratively imposed civil penalties based upon fraud, and there are several agencies that possess such authority. They, too, would now have to proceed judicially. But is the Court's opinion limited to cases claiming fraud? It states that "the remedy is all but dispositive,"[31] and the conclusion that the civil penalty is designed to punish and deter "effectively decides... this suit."[32] That is, the fact that the agency seeks a civil penalty is "all but dispositive" and "effectively decides" the right to a jury trial. The fact that the claim sounded in fraud merely "confirms that conclusion."[33] What then of *Atlas Roofing*? The Court's criticism of the case and the claims that it has been undermined may suggest it is ripe for overruling. Certainly, Justices Gorsuch and Thomas would support such an outcome. Such a conclusion would sound the death knell for the 200-odd administratively imposed civil penalty provisions in federal law. Moreover, OSHA does not have the ability to seek civil penalties in

---

[31] *Jarksey, supra* note 5, at 2129.
[32] *Ibid.*, at 2130.
[33] *Ibid.*

court; its statute only allows for civil penalties in administrative adjudications. Thus, overruling *Atlas Roofing* would effectively eliminate OSHA enforcement of the Occupational Safety and Health Act altogether.

There are even suggestions in the Court's opinion that Article III may require agencies to bring all enforcement cases in court, rather than administratively, unless the action falls within one of what the Court characterizes as the narrow, historical exceptions for "public rights" cases. The Court quotes from the ancient case of *Murray's Lessee v. Hoboken Land & Improvement Co.*, "we think it proper to state that we do not consider Congress can … withdraw from judicial cognizance any matter which, from its nature, is the subject of a suit at the common law, or in equity, or admiralty."[34] Again, this is something Justices Gorsuch and Thomas would support.

One potential hope for federal administrative adjudication of civil penalties would be the defendant's consent, because defendants' can waive their right to a jury trial. Agencies might file an administrative case against a defendant but allow for the person to remove the case to federal court, assuming the agency has the authority to bring judicial cases as well as administrative cases.[35] Defendants often might prefer the quicker and cheaper administrative adjudication. This work-around is not as simple as it sounds, however, because only the Department of Justice, not the enforcing agency, can authorize the judicial suit, and that authorization is not automatic.

Finally, while the Supreme Court did not reach two of the issues decided by the Fifth Circuit—that the removal protections for ALJs were unconstitutional and that the SEC's option to proceed either administratively or judicially violated the Delegation Doctrine—it did not vacate them, so that they remain the law within the Fifth Circuit. Ultimately, these issues will have to be decided by the Supreme Court, but for now they apply to cases brought within the Fifth Circuit.

---

[34] *Jarkesy*, *supra* note 5, at 2134 (quoting *Murray's Lessee v. Hoboken Land & Improvement Co.*, 18 How. 272, 284 (1856)).

[35] This has been suggested in Christopher J. Walker and David T. Zaring, *The Right to Remove in Agency Adjudication*, 85 Ohio State L.J. 1 (2024).

CHAPTER 8

Loper Bright v. Raimondo and *Relentless v. Department of Commerce*: The End of *Chevron* Deference

Carol Nackenoff and Avishai Greenberg

Federal administrative agencies have been having a rough time in the Supreme Court,[1] with environmental regulations a particular recent target.[2] And on June 28, 2024, the Court struck an even more significant blow to administrative agencies and the regulations they have promulgated in *Loper Bright v. Raimondo* and *Relentless v. Department of*

---

[1] The Department of Homeland Security is an exception, with two recent decisions upholding executive discretion in foreign affairs, See "*U.S. v. Texas* on State Challenges to Immigration Enforcement Policies," Ch. 15, *SCOTUS 2023* and "*Biden v. Texas* on Immigration Policy at the U.S.-Mexico Border," Ch. 12, *SCOTUS 2022.*

[2] See, for example, *Sackett v. EPA* (Sackett II, 2023), *Ohio v. EPA* (2024), and *West Virginia v. EPA* (2022).

C. Nackenoff (✉) · A. Greenberg
Swarthmore College, Swarthmore, PA, USA
e-mail: cnacken1@swarthmore.edu

A. Greenberg
e-mail: agreenb3@swarthmore.edu

© The Author(s), under exclusive license to Springer Nature Switzerland AG 2025
H. Schweber (ed.), *SCOTUS 2024*,
https://doi.org/10.1007/978-3-031-78551-1_8

Commerce. Erased was a forty year precedent, *Chevron U.S.A. v. Natural Resources Defense Council*, possibly the most cited Supreme Court administrative law decision of all time, relied upon by that Court seventy times and by lower federal courts about 18,000 times.[3] In the Court's *Loper Bright* decision, *Chevron* was overruled.[4]

When *Chevron* was decided in 1984, it was often held up as an exercise of judicial restraint, including by Justice Scalia,[5] who joined the unanimous (6–0) opinion. The Reagan Administration was attempting to loosen regulatory restrictions on businesses and was being rebuffed by the U.S. Circuit Court of Appeals in Washington, D.C. In *Chevron*, the Court upheld an industry-friendly ruling by EPA Administrator Anne Burford, Justice Gorsuch's mother. Since the Clean Air Act did not define "stationary source," the Court reasoned that the EPA's decision to allow a lenient, plantwide definition ("bubbling") was a permissible construction of the statutory term. "*Chevron* deference" meant that, when the statute did not expressly speak to the question at issue, and where the agency's interpretation did not clearly contradict the statutory provisions, a reasonable administrative determination or regulation deserved judicial deference.[6]

Chevron has come to be maligned by many conservatives. The three most recent Supreme Court nominees were questioned about *Chevron* in Senate hearings.[7] When serving on the 10th Circuit, Judge Gorsuch wrote that "*Chevron* seems no less than a judge-made doctrine for the abdication of the judicial duty."[8] Then D.C. Circuit Court of Appeals Judge Kavanaugh wrote that "*Chevron* encourages the Executive Branch

---

[3] 467 U.S. 837 (1984). Amy Howe, "Supreme Court Strikes Down *Chevron*, Curtailing the Power of Agencies," SCOTUSBlog, June 28, 2024; Peter M. Shane and Christopher J. Walker, "*Chevron* at Thirty: Looking Back and Looking Forward," *Fordham Law Review* 83, 2 (2014): 475, reporting it was the most cited administrative law decision up to that time.

[4] Chief Justice Roberts, majority opinion, *Loper Bright v. Raimondo*, 603 U.S. __ (2024). Slip opinion at 32–33, 35.

[5] Antonin Scalia, "Judicial Deference to Administrative Interpretations of Law," *Duke Law Journal* 1989, 3 (June): 511–521.

[6] Roberts, majority opinion, *Loper Bright*, slip opinion at 2.

[7] Senator Klobuchar's *Chevron* questions and the answers from all three recent nominees at https://www.klobuchar.senate.gov/public/index.cfm/2024/6/klobuchar-statement-following-the-supreme-court-decision-to-overturn-chevron-deference.

[8] *Gutierrez-Brizuela v. Lynch*, 834 F. 3d 1142, 1152 (10th Circuit 2016).

(whichever party controls it) to be extremely aggressive in seeking to squeeze its policy goals into ill-fitting statutory authorizations and restraints."[9]

The Roberts Court has avoided taking *Chevron* deference head-on and has abstained from applying it in recent years. It "has not deferred to an agency interpretation under *Chevron* since 2016."[10] Recent invocation of the "major questions" doctrine has been one means of invalidating federal regulations while sidestepping a *Chevron* confrontation. Using that doctrine, the Roberts Court held in *West Virginia v. EPA* (2022) that without clear statutory authorization from Congress, agency actions having vast "economic and political significance" cannot stand.[11] The decision invalidated the Obama Administration's Clean Power Plan, which relied on a section of the Clean Air Act.

BACKGROUND

Section 1853 of the Magnuson-Stevens Fishery Conservation and Management Act of 1976 [MSA] authorizes the National Marine Fisheries Service [NMFS] (part of the Department of Commerce) to "require that one or more observers be carried on board" a US fishing vessel operating within 200 nautical miles of the shore in an effort to prevent overfishing, The MSA created regional fishery management councils that must include in their plans "a mechanism for specifying annual catch limits… at a level such that overfishing does not occur."[12] The MSA specified certain groups that would have to pay costs for observers, but of the eight regional councils, only the North Pacific Council was named because so many of the largest commercial fishing enterprises operate there. The MSA did not specify that Atlantic herring fishermen had to pay the costs associated with any plan devised by the New England Fishery Management Council, and for a time, NMFS funded the observer coverage this council proposed and NMFS imposed in 2020. If NMFS

---

[9] Brett Kavanaugh, "Fixing Statutory Interpretation," *Harvard Law Review* 129 (2016), 2118, 2150.

[10] Roberts, majority opinion at 29.

[11] See R. Shep Melnick, "*West Virginia v. EPA* on Climate Change and Administrative Power," Ch. 11 in *SCOTUS 2022*; Jasmine Farrier, "*Biden v. Nebraska* and *Department of Education v. Brown*," Ch. 9 in SCOTUS 2023.

[12] Roberts, majority opinion at 2–3.

decides an observer is required and does not assign one paid by the government, the vessel has to arrange and pay for the observer, estimated to cost up to $710 per day while the vessel is at sea.[13]

In *Loper Bright*, a group of family businesses operating in the Atlantic herring fishery challenged the rule, arguing against the proposition that "under a proper application of *Chevron*, the MSA implicitly grants NMFS the power to force domestic vessels to pay the salaries of the monitors they must carry."[14] In *Relentless,* the owners of two fishing vessels that can freeze fish at sea, take longer trips of ten to fourteen days, and catch more species (therefore declaring into multiple fisheries each trip) challenged the same rule. If they seek to catch Atlantic herring, they must carry an observer if NMFS requires it.[15] *Relentless* owners asked "[w]hether the phrase 'necessary and appropriate' in the MSA augments agency power to force domestic fishing vessels to contract with and pay the salaries of federal observers they must carry."[16]

The District Court for the District of Columbia awarded summary judgment for the government in *Loper Bright* and the D.C. Circuit Court subsequently affirmed that decision. In *Relentless*, the District Court for Rhode Island granted summary judgment for NMFS and the First Circuit Court held that Congress had authorized NMFS to require monitors on boats and that it was reasonable to assume that the industry would pay. While all the lower courts relied on *Chevron* in finding for the government, they variously invoked step one or step two of *Chevron* two-step deference.

Relentless was likely added to the Supreme Court docket because Justice Jackson recused herself from *Loper Bright*, presumably because of her involvement at the district court level.[17] The Court granted certiorari

---

[13] Roberts, majority opinion at 3–4. The Court notes this could reduce the annual return to the vessel's owner by 20%.

[14] Loper Bright v. Raimondo, Petition for Writ of Certiorari at i; https://www.supremecourt.gov/DocketPDF/22/22-451/246256/20221110145441811_2022-11-10%20Loper%20Bright%20Cert%20Petition%20FINAL.pdf.

[15] Roberts, majority opinion at 5–6.

[16] Relentless Inc. v. U.S. Department of Commerce, Petition for Writ of Certiorari at ii; https://www.supremecourt.gov/DocketPDF/22/22-451/246256/20221110145441811_2022-11-10%20Loper%20Bright%20Cert%20Petition%20FINAL.pdf.

[17] Amy Howe, "Supreme Court to Hear Major Case on Power of Federal Agencies," SCOTUSBlog, January 16, 2024,

in both cases to consider whether the NMFS overstepped its authority and whether *Chevron* should be overruled.

Chevron did not mention Sect. 706 of the Administrative Procedure Act of 1946 [APA]. This section is best known for its arbitrary, capricious, or abuse of discretion standard for court rejection of administrative rules and regulations, and also—in environmental litigation involving citizen suits—the command that courts shall "compel agency action unlawfully withheld or unreasonably delayed." However, other language in the section directs courts to set aside agency action contrary to the Constitution or "in excess of statutory jurisdiction,"[18] and thus the APA would loom large in oral argument and the Court's majority opinion.

Oral Argument

Petitioners were represented without charge by two conservative legal groups linked to billionaire anti-regulation activist Charles Koch.[19] In separate cases argued the same day, oral arguments revolved around the justification for *Chevron* deference and the ramifications of eliminating it. The fishing companies argued that *Chevron* violates the Constitution by reallocating to administrative agencies the interpretive authority granted to courts by Article III. It further ignores and violates §706 of the APA, stating that "court[s] shall decide all relevant questions of law, interpret constitutional and statutory provisions, and determine the meaning or applicability of the terms of an agency action."[20] *Chevron*, they claimed, provided an unworkable test since different judges apply *Chevron* analysis differently; it was also a "reliance-destroying doctrine" since it allowed for the agencies to change their own interpretations of statutes whenever they desired.[21]

Solicitor General Prelogar argued in response that if Congress can authorize an agency to interpret the law through an express delegation,

---

[18] https://www.law.cornell.edu/uscode/text/5/706.

[19] Howe, "Supreme Court strikes down Chevron."

[20] https://uscode.house.gov/view.xhtml?req=granuleid:USC-2000-title5-section706&num=0&edition=2000.

[21] *Relentless* oral argument transcript at 24; https://www.supremecourt.gov/oral_arguments/argument_transcripts/2023/22-1219_e2p3.pdf.

it can also do so implicitly.[22] Further, APA §706 does not prescribe a universal standard of review for statutory interpretation questions.[23] An agency's ability to change positions allows it to adapt regulations according to changes on the ground, thus making it more reliable.[24] Prelogar emphasized that ignoring *stare decisis* by eliminating *Chevron* would undermine dozens of Supreme Court, and thousands of lower court, decisions. Congress, agencies, courts, and the American public have relied on *Chevron* for 40 years; upending the doctrine would cause a tremendous shock to the country's legal system.

Questions from the bench focused on constitutionality, reliance, workability, and *stare decisis*. Justices Kagan, Jackson, and Sotomayor voiced concerns that without *Chevron*, courts would become "uber-legislators."[25] They feared that policy decisions would be made by courts in cases where there existed real ambiguity that should be resolved by a politically accountable branch of government. They were sympathetic to Prelogar's argument that without *Chevron*, reliance interests would be frustrated. Justice Jackson worried that many regulations would not be implemented by agencies as legal challenges worked their way through hundreds of district courts, creating major issues of workability.[26] Justice Kagan saw both *Chevron* and *stare decisis* as "doctrine[s] of humility"; doing away with them would lead people to no longer think "the courts are acting like courts."[27]

While the Solicitor General claimed it would be more unworkable not to have *Chevron* and have every circuit court offer a different interpretation instead of allowing the agency to make a nationwide decision,[28] Justice Gorsuch warned that *Chevron* deference created a situation in which "each new administration can come in and undo the work of a prior

---

[22] Solicitor General Prelogar, *Loper Bright* oral argument transcript at 48; https://www.supremecourt.gov/oral_arguments/argument_transcripts/2023/22-451_o7jp.pdf.

[23] Solicitor General Prelogar, *Relentless* oral argument transcript at 77.

[24] *Loper Bright* oral argument transcript at 84–85.

[25] Term used by Justice Jackson in *Relentless* oral argument transcript at 69.

[26] *Relentless* oral argument transcript at 73, 80.

[27] *Loper Bright* oral argument transcript at 35.

[28] *Relentless* oral argument transcript at 73.

one."²⁹ Justices Kavanaugh and Alito also considered *Chevron* unworkable because it required judges to determine when a statute is ambiguous or not, and seemed to agree with Justice Gorsuch that the "ambiguous ambiguity trigger" in *Chevron* led to inconsistent lower court decisions.³⁰

Justice Barrett raised a concern that overturning *Chevron* would mean "inviting a flood of litigation," challenging all cases decided under the doctrine in the last forty years. Petitioners claimed that overturning *Chevron* would not overturn the decisions in those cases.

Opinion of the Court

Chief Justice Roberts wrote the majority opinion and was joined by Justices Thomas, Alito, Gorsuch, Kavanaugh, and Barrett.³¹ The Roberts opinion focused on the incompatibility of the APA with *Chevron*.

The majority declared that "[t]he deference that *Chevron* requires of courts reviewing agency action cannot be squared with the APA."³² Courts are charged with construing the meaning of statutes, and despite ambiguity, "there is a best reading all the same... It therefore makes no sense to speak of a 'permissible' interpretation that is not the one the court, after applying all relevant interpretive tools, concludes is best. In the business of statutory interpretation, if it is not the best, it is not permissible."³³

Emphasizing its adherence to the APA, the Court stressed that Congress may still delegate discretionary authority to agencies, as it sometimes has to interpret particular statutory terms, and that courts will accept such delegations that remain within constitutional bounds.³⁴ And agency interpretations still "constitute a body of experience and

---

²⁹ *Ibid* at 93–94.

³⁰ *Loper Bright* oral argument transcript at 24, 53.

³¹ Justice Thomas, in a separate concurrence, argued that *Chevron* deference violates the Constitution's separation of powers, giving power to agencies that is constitutionally granted only to courts (Thomas concurrence at 2, 4). Justice Gorsuch's concurrence examined the proper use of *stare decisis* and contended that *Chevron* "did not merely depart from our precedents. More nearly, *Chevron* defied them,,,." *Chevron* was a "startling development" that we are "bound to inter." (Gorsuch concurrence at 17, 34).

³² Roberts, majority opinion at 18.

³³ *Ibid* at 23.

³⁴ Roberts, majority opinion at 17, 26, 27.

informed judgment" that may be "entitled to respect."[35] When it delegates, however, Congress should do so expressly; otherwise, agencies have a self-interest in interpreting their mandate broadly.[36] "By forcing courts to... pretend that ambiguities are necessarily delegations, *Chevron* does not prevent judges from making policy. It prevents them from judging."[37]

Chief Justice Roberts characterized the Court's forty-year history with the precedent as "imposing one limitation on *Chevron* after another" that came to involve a "byzantine set of preconditions and exceptions."[38] *Chevron* is not the sort of "'stable background' rule" that fosters meaningful reliance. It is unworkable; ambiguity evades meaningful definition. And "*[s]tare decisis* is not an 'inexorable command.'" The *Chevron* project "has proved to be fundamentally misguided."[39] It has "become an impediment, rather than an aid, to accomplishing the basic judicial task of 'say[ing] what the law is.'"[40]

In overruling *Chevron*, the majority concluded that "Courts must exercise their independent judgment in deciding whether an agency has acted within its statutory authority, as the APA requires." Yet the decision was explicit in not calling into question earlier cases that had relied on the *Chevron* framework; a challenge would require some special justification.[41]

Dissent

Justice Kagan penned the dissent, joined by Justices Sotomayor and Jackson. She lamented the Court's decision to turn the Court into "the country's administrative czar" by having it decide issues no matter how "expertise-driven or policy-laden" they are.[42] She rejected the majority's premise that looking at judicial history proves the APA was meant

---

[35] *Skidmore v. Swift & Co.*, 323 U.S. 134, 140 (1944), majority opinion at 16–17, 25.
[36] Roberts, majority opinion at 23.
[37] Ibid at 26, 27.
[38] Ibid at 28.
[39] Ibid at 29, 30.
[40] Ibid at 32.
[41] Ibid at 34.
[42] Kagan dissent at 3.

to ensure courts were not deferential to agencies. Justice Kagan emphasized that §706 of the APA "does not specify *any* standard of review for construing statutes" and so does not preclude *Chevron* deference.[43]

Justice Kagan criticized the Court's treatment of precedent, asserting that "*Chevron* is entitled to a particularly strong form of *stare decisis*" since Congress has not challenged *Chevron* for decades (e.g., by amending the APA), and since overturning *Chevron* means overturning not one decision, but many.[44] The dissent also criticized the Court's disregard for judicial humility, warning that the decision is part of a wider worrisome Court trend in its treatment of agencies and precedent.[45]

Implications

While the decision immediately impacts the NMFS, many agencies have reason to be concerned with the implications of *Chevro*n's demise. Liberals point to the likely impact on regulations promoting clean air and water, environmental protection, food safety, and health care costs.[46] Opponents of the administrative state are generally pleased that no longer will *Chevron* deference be used "to justify expansion of the agency's mission."[47] And many business interests welcome curbing agencies' ability to rewrite regulations as different parties control the White House.

In one regard, change may not be drastic, since the Supreme Court had not relied on *Chevron* since 2016 and the outcome in *Loper Bright* has been widely expected—including by administrative agencies.[48] There may possibly be a silver lining in *Loper Bright* as well: The decision may

---

[43] *Ibid* at 16 (her emphasis).

[44] *Ibid* at 25.

[45] *Ibid* at 32.

[46] *Ibid* at 2 and 28. David Ovalle, Joel Achenbach, and Rachel Roubein, "How the Supreme Court has roiled U.S. health-care agencies," *Washington Post*, (July 2, 2024); https://www.washingtonpost.com/health/2024/07/02/chevron-doctrine-fda-public-health-supreme-court/.

[47] Bob Egelko, "The Supreme Court Appears Poised to Overturn a Ruling Cited in More Than 19,000 Cases," *San Francisco Chronicle*, updated May 17, 2023, quoting Michael McConnell.

[48] Nina H. Farah, Lesley Clark, and E&E News, "How a Landmark Supreme Court Decision Will Reshape the U.S. Energy Sector," *Scientific American*, (July 1, 2024); https://www.scientificamerican.com/article/how-the-supreme-courts-chevron-def erence-ruling-could-remake-the-energy/.

reduce or eliminate the need for the Court's ill-defined, recent "major questions" doctrine.[49]

As courts are urged to look more closely at agency interpretations of statutes, many more challenges to administrative rules and regulations are sure to follow. Justice Barrett is probably correct: *Loper Bright* and *Relentless* may open the Court to a flood of cases in the coming years—an expectation shared by some legal experts.[50] Despite the Court's refusal to call into question earlier cases using the *Chevron* framework, the requirement of some additional reason to challenge decisions that used *Chevron* may not be a high barrier. Justice Kagan stated that although the majority is "sanguine" in regard to previous *Chevron*-based decisions being challenged, she is "not so much." Courts so motivated "can always come up with something to label a 'special justification.'"[51]

Some practitioners and legal scholars echo Justice Kagan's fears of what is to come.[52] Environmentalists are concerned because many of the regulations promulgated by the EPA rely on older statutes (such as the Clean Air Act and Clean Water Act), which have been applied to modern problems they were not originally written to specifically address; *Loper Bright* makes some of these regulations much harder to justify.[53] It will also be harder to justify regulatory changes based on technological breakthroughs.[54] The litigation director for the Southern Environmental Law Center, reacting to *Loper Bright*, said: "hundreds of federal judges—who lack the expertise of agency personnel—are certain to reach inconsistent results on the meaning of federal laws as applied to complex, technical issues."[55]

---

[49] Richard J. Pierce, Jr., "Two Neglected Effects of Loper Bright," *Regulatory Review* (July 1, 2024); Cary Coglianese, "Questions Remain on Major Questions Doctrine," (June 30, 2023); https://www.law.upenn.edu/live/news/15982-questions-remain-on-major-questions-doctrine.

[50] Farah, Clark, and E&E News, *supra* note 48.

[51] Kagan, dissent at 31.

[52] Farah, Clark, and E&E News, *supra* note 48.

[53] This includes categorizing greenhouse gasses as air pollutants. Zoë Schlanger, "American Environmentalism Just Got Shoved Into Legal Purgatory," *The Atlantic*, June 28, (2024), https://www.theatlantic.com/science/archive/2024/06/chevron-overruled-environmental-regulation/678843/.

[54] Farah, Clark, and E&E News, *supra* note 48.

[55] Howe, "Supreme Court Strikes Down Chevron," quoting Kym Meyer.

The majority engages in a textualist premise that there is one best reading of a statute's meaning and insists that judges have an expertise and neutrality in interpreting the law that policymakers do not. This clearly locates more power in the judicial branch at a time when the Roberts Court has not been reticent to overturn or limit statutes and curb executive power in other domestic policy arenas.

CHAPTER 9

Ohio v. Environmental Protection Agency: The Emergency Docket Shapes National Policy Again

Julie Novkov

In a term with multiple major cases addressing the shape and scope of the administrative state, the Court's emergency docket ruling in *Ohio v. Environmental Protection Agency* temporarily pausing a not-yet-fully-implemented environmental rule may seem technical and less consequential. The majority's approach, however, reinforces a template for pausing regulations prior to full judicial review. It also underlines the trend of assigning more power to the courts to manage and calibrate administrative regulation. This chapter provides some background on the Clean Air Act and describes how the EPA works with states to meet air quality standards. It then turns to the details and implications of this dispute.

J. Novkov (✉)
Rockefeller College of Public Affairs & Policy, University at Albany, SUNY, Albany, NY, USA
e-mail: jnovkov@albany.edu

The Clean Air Act of 1970, a landmark national environmental law, establishes a partnership between the states and the federal government to limit harmful emissions, placing federal regulatory authority in the hands of the Environmental Protection Agency (EPA). The Act makes states responsible for limiting emissions within their borders to meet federal air quality standards. However, states cannot control emissions produced in other states. The flow of harmful emissions across state lines (deemed "interstate transport") thus poses problems for states located downwind of other states that produce greater emissions, since the downwind states may find themselves exceeding federal standards from emissions generated outside of their borders. The Clean Air Act thus includes a "Good Neighbor" provision that "requires states to prohibit emissions that significantly contribute to air quality problems in another state" (Shouse 2018, 1). The EPA sets national standards for air pollutants and the states are responsible for designing policies to meet these standards, generating individual state implementation plans (SIP) (Shouse 2018, 3–4).

In 2015, the EPA revised its standards for ozone, a component of smog that damages living cells in humans, other animals, and plants. After the revision, states were required to submit their SIPs by 2018, explaining how they would meet the new, stricter standards. While several states submitted plans, some did not, and some that did so claimed that they did not have to adopt provisions to address potential downwind emissions or that no further cost-efficient measures could be undertaken. In February of 2022, the EPA disapproved 19 of the state SIPs for not addressing their Good Neighbor obligations sufficiently, adding four more disapprovals shortly afterward (Ohio v. Environmental Protection Agency 2024, 603:3–4). In February 2023, the EPA finalized the disapprovals of the SIPs and followed up by finalizing a federal Good Neighbor Plan that applied to 23 states, 21 of which had disapproved plans and two that had not revised their plans (Bowers 2024, 2).

The new Good Neighbor Plan "establish[ed] an allowance-based nitrogen oxide emissions trading program" for which each state had a "budget of permissible emissions," with the initial budget being based on "immediately available measures." The budget was slated to tighten over time to reduce emissions, requiring annual analysis. The Plan also identified specific emissions requirements for industries with high emission rates. Both the Plan and the SIP rejections sparked lawsuits across the country, with states objecting in the Fourth, Fifth, Sixth, Eighth, Ninth, Tenth, and Eleventh circuits to their plans' denials and several states and trade associations challenging the Good Neighbor Plan in the D.C. circuit (Bowers 2024, 3–4). On the SIP side, circuit courts in twelve states stayed the EPA's denial (Ohio v. Environmental Protection Agency 2024, 603:8). In conjunction with these challenges, litigants requested that the court enjoin the implementation of the federal Good Neighbor Plan while the litigation proceeded. On September 25, 2023, the D.C. Circuit declined to stay the plan, sparking an appeal to the U.S. Supreme Court (Bowers 2024, 4).

The Supreme Court's ruling

The posture of the case was unusual. No final decision had been rendered regarding the fate of either the SIPs or the Plan. The litigants nonetheless sought to block the implementation of the federal Plan prior to its substantive judicial review. They claimed that, with so many states pulled out of the Good Neighbor Plan because of the legal uncertainty around their SIPs, enforcement of the federal Plan against them would meet the Clean Air Act's standard for reversal: that the EPA's action was arbitrary or capricious. Although the case was not debated on the merits, the Court considered more than 400 pages of technical briefing in addition to the record and the oral argument.[1]

The Justices ruled in a 5–4 split to stay the enforcement of the Good Neighbor Plan until the legal challenges brought by the various state had been resolved. The opinion, written by noted critic of the administrative state Neil Gorsuch, considered the established questions to determine whether a stay was appropriate: (1) whether the litigants requesting the stay were likely to prevail on the merits of the case, (2) whether stay applicants risked irreparable injury without a pause in the litigation, (3) whether staying the litigation would "substantially injure" other interested parties, and (4) where public interest concerns weighed.[2] After a very brief analysis, the opinion concluded that "because each side has strong arguments about the harms they face and the equities involved, our resolution of these stay requests ultimately turns on the merits and the question of who is likely to prevail at the end of this litigation."[3] It

---

[1] *Ohio v. Environmental Protection Agency*, 603 US ___, No. 23A349, slip op. at 8–9.

[2] *Id.*, slip op. at 10.

[3] *Id.*, slip op. at 11.

then turned to an analysis of whether a court would ultimately determine that the final federal Plan was arbitrary or capricious, concluding that the litigants challenging the rule could indeed make this showing. Thus, while the Court's decision did not reach a ruling on the merits, it contained a strong indication that the majority expects the challenges to the EPA's actions to succeed.

The problem for the majority was in the uncertainties in the state plans' status and how these uncertainties affected the federal Good Neighbor Plan. The Plan, explained the Court, was based on the presumption that 23 states covered by the Plan would adopt policies to drive emissions down to meet the federal standards. Since the EPA's Plan relied on states' individual plans and several states were either not covered by the federal plan or were challenging the EPA's rejection of their plans, the EPA "could not represent with certainty whether the cost-effectiveness analysis it performed collectively for 23 States would yield the same results and command the same emissions-control measures if conducted for, say, just one State."[4] This uncertainty led the Court to conclude that the final rule was not reasonably explained and that the EPA had ignored an important aspect of the problem. On this basis, the Court concluded that the Good Neighbor Plan was ultimately unlikely to survive review.

The Court rejected the EPA's defenses. The EPA included a provision acknowledging that some states might be left out of the system, mandating that the Plan could nonetheless move forward. To the Court, however, the inclusion of this severability provision simply indicated that the EPA recognized the challengers' concerns and chose to sidestep them rather than address them. To succeed, "EPA needed to explain why it believed its rule would continue to offer cost-effective improvements in downwind air quality with only a subset of the States it originally intended to cover."[5] The EPA also objected that the specific concerns embraced by the Court were not raised during the public comment period. The Court disagreed, reading some comments as raising the possibility that states' removal from the Plan would require an entirely new assessment.[6] Finally, the Court dismissed the EPA's objection that the proper path to

---

[4] *Id.*, slip op. at 12–13.

[5] *Id.*, slip op. at 14.

[6] *Id.*, slip op. at 15.

challenge the final rule was to do so through asking the EPA to reconsider it rather than seeking judicial intervention. In the majority's view, the EPA had simply "failed to address an important problem the public could and did raise during the comment period."[7]

The 5–4 split featured a dissent authored by Amy Coney Barrett and joined by Justices Sotomayor, Kagan, and Jackson. The unusual configuration of Justices united behind Justice Barrett's objection that the Court improperly granted emergency relief "in a fact-intensive and highly technical case without fully engaging with both the relevant law and voluminous record."[8] In the dissenters' view, the Court failed to appreciate the EPA's leading responsibility to ensure that States meet air-quality standards. The dissent emphasized the EPA's statutory leadership role and noted that its disapproval of the SIPs, despite the challenges, might indeed have been proper. They objected to the majority's description of the concerns raised in the comment period and explained the Good Neighbor Plan as a holistic effort to reduce emissions.[9]

Far from concluding that EPA's actions were arbitrary and capricious, the dissenters doubted that the challenge would succeed when fully briefed and argued on the merits on procedural grounds. A lawsuit challenging a rule issued under the Clean Air Act can proceed only if the objection to the rule was presented during the comment period. The Clean Air Act mandates that new concerns recognized or raised after the adoption of a rule should result first in a petition to EPA to ask the agency to reconsider; only after this procedural step would a lawsuit be appropriate.[10] In the dissenters' view, the turn to the courts was thus premature.

The dissenters also read the arbitrary and capricious standard as raising a high barrier for a successful challenge. Justice Barrett noted that agency decisions need not be ideal or pose perfect solutions for problems. The proper yardstick for her was reasonableness, and she argued that the Plan's reliance on nationwide data for emissions was reasonable. Unlike the majority, she took the severance provision as further evidence of reasonableness on the EPA's part, providing needed flexibility to ensure

---

[7] *Id.*, slip op. at 17.

[8] *Id.*, slip op. at 1 (Barrett, J.).

[9] *Id.*, slip op. at 5 (Barrett, J.).

[10] *Id.*, slip op. at 6 (Barrett, J.).

effective implementation and reliance by stakeholders.[11] Reflecting a deeper disagreement, Justice Barrett described the process as a proper reflection of Congress's will to empower an agency to make expert decisions and consider and evaluate public concerns. Furthermore, Congress had reinforced its intent by incorporating a "stringent harmless-error rule," allowing courts to invalidate an EPA rule "if the errors were *so serious* and related to matters of *such central relevance* to the rule that there is a *substantial likelihood* that the rule would have been *significantly changed* if such errors had not been made."[12] The concerns raised in the litigation did not meet this standard, leading the dissenters to conclude the success on the merits was unlikely.

THE SIGNIFICANCE OF THE STAY

For a Court that created the major questions doctrine and overturned *Chevron*, the implications of this ruling may seem less than momentous.[13] A majority is skeptical about EPA's justifications for the Good Neighbor Rule and seems inclined to grant *certiorari* to invalidate it after the lower courts have weighed in. But the Rule's final fate as well as the fate of the SIPs under challenge must be determined through lengthy and technical proceedings that will establish factual determinations about a bewildering array of emissions sources and the implications of potentially uneven state-level regulation. As we saw in *West Virginia v. EPA*,[14] by the time a final resolution is sought in the Supreme Court, the entire dispute may be in the rearview mirror due to a change of administration and agency direction, further developments in technology and industry response to climate concerns, or both. The ruling nonetheless has two important implications beyond its impact on efforts to regulate greenhouse gas emissions.

The Court's decision to intervene and the way that it intervened in this case are striking for two reasons. First, the Court opted to produce a full ruling prior to the lower court's having concluded its factfinding

---

[11] *Id.*, slip op. at 17 (Barrett, J.).

[12] *Id.*, slip op. at 19–20 (Barrett, J.). Emphasis Barrett's.

[13] See discussion of *Loper Bright v. Raimondo* in Chapter 11 of this volume.

[14] *West Virginia v. Environmental Protection Agency*, 597 U.S. ___, No. 20–1530 (2022).

around the substantive issues and without having available a fully developed factual and procedural record. The uncertainty is magnified because litigation over the Good Neighbor Plan is proceeding alongside numerous ongoing suits regarding individual SIPs that could, upon their resolution at the trial level, provoke appeals. As Steve Vladeck has noted, in the last few years, the Court has been increasingly inclined to use these types of intermediate proceedings to resolve major policy questions, issuing decisions with national impacts (Vladeck 2023).

Second, the Court further underlined its portrayal of the federal courts generally and the Supreme Court in particular as front-line experts who properly hold the authority to evaluate and decide complex questions about scientific facts and technological capacity. While *Loper Bright Enterprises*' overruling of *Chevron* deference is the most influential ruling embracing this agenda, the Court's handling of this case provides a model for similar challenges in the future. In *Ohio v. EPA*, the Court signals that those who object to regulations need not wait until legal challenges have played out to prevent their implementation. Under the right circumstances, a quick mini-trial before the Justices may be enough.

Bibliography

Bowers, Kate. 2024. "Supreme Court to Consider Request to Stay EPA's Good Neighbor Interstate Air Pollution Rule." LSB11107. Washington, DC: Congressional Research Service.

Ohio v. Environmental Protection Agency. 2024, 603 U.S. US Supreme Court.

Shouse, Kate. 2018. "The Clean Air Act's Good Neighbor Provision: Overview of Interstate Air Pollution Control." 7–5700. Washington, DC: Congressional Research Service. https://sgp.fas.org/crs/misc/R45299.pdf.

Vladeck, Stephen. 2023. *The Shadow Docket: How the Supreme Court Uses Stealth Rulings to Amass Power and Undermine the Republic*. New York, NY: Basic Books.

CHAPTER 10

NetChoice v. *Paxton*: Navigating and Refereeing Freedom of Speech in Cyberspace

Mark Rush

In *NetChoice* v. *Paxton* and the companion case *Moody* v. *NetChoice*, a unanimous Supreme Court essentially told *NetChoice* and the Fifth and Eleventh Circuits to go back and do their homework. Speaking for the Court, Justice Kagan stated:

> NetChoice must show that the law at issue (whether from Texas or from Florida) prohibits a substantial amount of protected speech relative to its plainly legitimate sweep. None of the parties below focused on that issue; nor did the Fifth or Eleventh Circuits....Even in the First Amendment context, facial challenges are disfavored, and neither parties nor courts can disregard the requisite inquiry into how a law works in all of its applications. So on remand, each court must evaluate the full scope of the law's

M. Rush (✉)
Washington and Lee University, Lexington, VA, USA
e-mail: rushm@wlm.edu

© The Author(s), under exclusive license to Springer Nature Switzerland AG 2025
H. Schweber (ed.), *SCOTUS 2024*,
https://doi.org/10.1007/978-3-031-78551-1_10

coverage. It must then decide which of the law's applications are constitutionally permissible and which are not, and finally weigh the one against the other.[1]

To guide the lower courts when they heard NetChoice's challenges again, the court majority restated its vision of how the First Amendment applies in a digital era and in the context of cyberspace. In so doing, I argue, it did more to muddy the waters than it did to offer clear guidance to the Fifth and Eleventh Circuits. The majority's discussion of the scope of the First Amendment is myopic and rooted in antiquated notions of free speech and the role the government must play in refereeing conflicts among rights-bearing individuals. In short, it fails to take into account the full impact of technological change on the "marketplace of ideas."

Clearly, the majority did not turn a blind eye to the impact of technology. But, it argued, enduring principles of First Amendment analysis still control its approach to free speech questions:

> [W]hatever the challenges of applying the Constitution to ever-advancing technology, the "basic principles" of the First Amendment "do not vary." New communications media differ from old ones in a host of ways: No one thinks Facebook's News Feed much resembles an insert put in a billing envelope. And similarly, today's social media pose dangers not seen earlier: No one ever feared the effects of newspaper opinion pages on adolescents' mental health. But analogies to old media, even if imperfect, can be useful. And better still as guides to decision are settled principles about freedom of expression, including the ones just described. Those principles have served the Nation well over many years, even as one communications method has given way to another. And they have much to say about the laws at issue here.[2]

Alas, the majority did little to move beyond what remains an essentially early 20th-century vision of liberties and the role of the state in playing referee among rights-bearing individuals. As I discuss below, the majority's vision of the "marketplace of ideas" compares to the vision of the economic marketplace that informed its early 20th century decisions. Until it refined that vision in 1937, the court evinced an absolute distrust of governmental involvement in the economic market. It then embraced

---

[1] Slip op. 30. Internal citations omitted.

[2] Slip op. 19–20. Internal citations omitted.

the need for government to play referee and ensure that the free market remained truly "free."

This was not lost on Justice Alito. While he supported the decision to remand the cases, he (and Justice Thomas who joined his concurrence) disagreed with the majority's analysis of the scope and definition of speech rights. From the perspective of the individual speaker, the threat posed to freedom of speech by the government or the platforms is essentially the same. The majority, however, focuses only on the threat posed by the government and overlooks the necessary role it must play in counterbalancing the impact of powerful private interests.

As well, the *NetChoice* majority struggled to embrace the dual role played by platforms. On the one hand, it regards them essentially as newspapers that collect news and express editorial opinions. But, it does not address the fact that platforms are much more: they operate as gatekeepers to the public square. As a result, they play the same censorial role that the claim the government is trying to play—but they are not electorally accountable.

The Texas and Florida Laws

Lawmakers in Texas and Florida passed laws to restrict the capacity of social media platforms to censor the speech of their users in response to the decision by Twitter and other platforms to shut down the account of then-President Donald Trump in the wake of the January 6, 2021 riot at the U.S. Capitol.[3] NetChoice contended that the laws essentially forced it to speak and express opinions that it did not support: "Texas's law requires the platforms to carry and promote speech that they would rather discard or downplay. The platforms object that the law thus forces them to alter the content of their expression—a particular compilation of third party speech."[4]

In this respect, the Court compared NetChoice's complaint to that made in 1974 by *The Miami Herald* in *Miami Herald Publishing Co. v. Tornillo*.[5] There, Florida had passed a law requiring the *Herald* to provide

---

[3] Slip op. 6–7. See also: https://www.npr.org/2024/07/01/nx-s1-4991108/supreme-court-NetChoice#:~:text=The%20Supreme%20Court%20on%20Monday%20put%20a%20pair,in%20doing%20so%2C%20it%20prompted%20five%20separate%20opinions.

[4] Slip op. 13–14.

[5] 418 U.S. 241 (1974).

rebuttal space to politicians that it criticized. The Court struck down the law, arguing that editorial judgment was a key component of the First Amendment: "The choice of material to go into a newspaper, and the decisions made as to limitations on the size and content of the paper, and treatment of public issues and public officials—whether fair or unfair—constitute the exercise of editorial control and judgment."[6] In *NetChoice* Justice Kagan, writing for the majority, concluded that forcing a platform to convey content that it wished to ban was the equivalent of forcing the paper to print speech with which it did not agree.

> [T]he major social-media platforms are in the business, when curating their feeds, of combining "multifarious voices" to create a distinctive expressive offering. The individual messages may originate with third parties, but the larger offering is the platform's. It is the product of a wealth of choices about whether—and, if so, how—to convey posts having a certain content or viewpoint ... Consider again an opinion page editor... who wants to publish a variety of views, but thinks some things off-limits (or, to change the facts, worth only a couple of column inches). The choice of material, the decisions made [as to] content, the treatment of public issues—whether fair or unfair—all these constitute the exercise of editorial control and judgment. For a paper, and for a platform too.[7]

The Court acknowledged the unique and powerful role played by newspapers in 1974 and platforms today. In the same way that, 50 years ago, "modern media empires had gained ever greater capacity to shape and even manipulate popular opinion,"[8] the *NetChoice* Court noted the powerful role platforms made in controlling access to and the dissemination of information. But, as in *Miami Herald*, the *NetChoice* court affirmed that "the cure proposed, [constraining editorial discretion], collided with the First Amendment's antipathy to *state* manipulation of the speech market."[9]

The majority's narrow focus on the threat posed by state regulation of the marketplace of ideas blinded it to the fact that the state also must play a critical role in refereeing that market. In the marketplace of speech the

---

[6] *Ibid.*, 258.

[7] Slip op. 24, internal citations omitted.

[8] Slip op. 14 citing 418 U.S. 241 at 249–250.

[9] Slip op. 14.

more powerful voices of the press and the media have always been able to drown out weaker voices simply by virtue of their capacity to broadcast information more powerfully and to a broader audience and to the extent that, once upon a time, the broadcast spectrum was limited.[10] Therefore, a limited number of actors could gain access to scarce broadcast spectrum space or dedicate the capital to compete with entities such as the *New York Times*. The vast scope of the internet might seem to resolve the problem of scarcity.[11] In fact, this is not the case. The correspondingly vast power of platform operators offers correspondingly vast *private* threats to individual speech rights and the diversity of the marketplace of ideas in ways that have no analogies in older forms of media. Accordingly, in a huge, expanding marketplace populated by correspondingly powerful private actors, it is necessary to empower the government with the capacity and tools necessary to play its role of referee. If the government is not so empowered, then powerful private actors will dominate weaker ones.

The Court's Oversights

In his concurrence, Justice Alito raised key issues that the majority overlooked. First, he emphasized that not all aspects of platform activity constitute messaging. To the extent that a platform can be compared to a parade or an edited anthology and, therefore, the platform is a "compiler" of third-party speech, it is entitled to editorial discretion. But, there is a difference between serving as a "curator" of particular information (which is an expressive function) and serving as a "dump pipe" which merely emits what it is fed.[12] Accordingly, whereas *Tornillo* drives the court's opinion because it compares platforms to newspapers, *Pruneyard Shopping Center v. Robins*[13] informs Alito because he compares platforms to shopping malls.[14]

---

[10] See, e.g., Fiss, Owen Fiss. 1986. "Free Speech and Social Structure." 71 Iowa Law Review 1405-25.

[11] See Volokh, Eugene. 1995. "Cheap Speech and What it Will Do." 104 Yale Law Journal 1805-50; Volokh, Eugene. 2021. "What Cheap Speech has Done: (Greater) Equality and its Discontents." 54 UC Davis Law Review 2303-40.

[12] Slip op. Alito concurring, 17.

[13] 447 U.S. 74 (1980).

[14] *Ibid.*, 20.

In *Pruneyard,* a California court ruled that the California constitution prevented a shopping mall from banning pamphleteers handing out handbills on the mall grounds. The Supreme Court held that this operation of the California constitution did not violate the First Amendment to the U.S. Constitution. To the extent that malls are private spaces that are open to the public, a state may regulate the owners' capacity to ban certain speakers (the analysis would have been the same if a California statute had been at issue). This is due, in part, to the fact that there is little probability that shopping mall owners will be perceived as endorsing the opinions of pamphleteers on their grounds. Allowing pamphleteers access to mall grounds is no more the equivalent of forced speech than allowing someone to walk around a mall or park wearing his "Fuck the Draft" t-shirt constitutes an endorsement of his opinions by the mall.[15] As a result, a state's compelling a mall owner to permit such expression does not entail the government compelling the owner to express a message with which he disagrees.

Second, and perhaps more important, Alito approached the facts in *NetChoice* from the perspective of the individual who is seeking access to the marketplace of ideas and who can do so only through or with the assistance of another party—such as a platform. In this respect, he echoed the court's decision in *Packingham* v. *North Carolina.*[16] There state had sought to cut off convicted sex offenders' access to the internet in order to distance them from potential victims. The Court ruled that "social-media platforms have become the modern public square to which everyone has a right of access."[17] "While in the past there may have been difficulty in identifying the most important places (in a spatial sense) for the exchange of views, today the answer is clear. It is cyberspace—the vast democratic forums of the Internet in general, and social media in particular."[18]

In keeping with the distinction made by the court in *NetChoice,* the *Packingham* court spoke only to *state* action to curtail access to the internet since the state of North Carolina had acted to restrict Packingham's access. But the Court's logic applies to *NetChoice* as well. If access

---

[15] *Cohen v. California,* 403 U.S. 15 (1971).

[16] 582 U.S. 98 (2017).

[17] Slip op. Alito concurring, 3. Citing 582 U.S. 98, 107 (2017).

[18] *Packingham,* 104. Internal citations removed.

to the internet is a fundamental part of free speech, how can it be constitutional for a private actor to restrict that same access if the state cannot? After all, if a private actor tries to prevent someone from speaking in a park the government has an obligation to protect that speaker against the threat of a "heckler's veto." In *Packingham*, Justice Kennedy asserted: "to foreclose access to social media altogether is to prevent the user from engaging in the legitimate exercise of First Amendment rights."[19] From the perspective of the silenced individual, Alito argued, the court's reasoning in the two cases is contradictory. The impact on speech rights is the same and it does not matter whose hand is curtailing liberty. Liberty is curtailed either way.

Perspective

The court's free speech case law compares to its *Lochner*[20] era decisions between 1890 and 1937 concerning property rights and the rights of labor. The *Lochner* Court manifested a pathological fear of government interference in the economic marketplace. The fear was so vast that it blinded the Court to the impact of and control exercised by powerful private actors. Accordingly, the Court endorsed a vision of the market that ignored the fact that if more powerful players were free to assert their liberties at the expense of weaker players, the market would simply favor the interests of the more powerful. The "general welfare"[21] would not permit the state to protect the interests of the weak.[22]

The court finally embraced the rights of weaker actors when it reversed course and, in cases such as *West Coast Hotel v. Parrish*, rearticulated the notion of economic liberty to include the legitimate interests of employees as well as employers and acknowledge the need for government to play referee between the strong and the weak.

> The Constitution...speaks of liberty and prohibits the deprivation of liberty without due process of law...But the liberty safeguarded is liberty in a social organization which requires the protection of law against the evils which

---

[19] *Packingham*, 108.

[20] *Lochner v. New York* 198 U.S. 45 (1905).

[21] U.S. Constitution, Art. I., section 8.

[22] See Genevieve Lakier, "The First Amendment's Real *Lochner* Problem." 87 *University of Chicago Law Review* 1241–1343 (2020).

menace the health, safety, morals and welfare of the people. Liberty under the Constitution is thus necessarily subject to the restraints of due process, and regulation which is reasonable in relation to its subject and is adopted in the interests of the community is due process.[23]

Alito's assertion that government regulation is necessary to balance the interests of weaker and stronger private actors reflects that of the Court in *Parrish*. Leaving platform operators free to censor their users' speech essentially outsources governmental censorial power to unaccountable private actors in the same way that denying government protections to empoyees endangered them in *Lochner*. The result is that weaker speakers cannot express themselves without the threat of censorship by others. Nor can they access the public square without the permission of powerful private actors. In this respect, the Court ends up undermining its goal of ensuring a free and open marketplace of ideas by letting powerful actors assert censorial power while denying the government the ability to play referee.

In essence, the difference of opinion between Alito and the majority is driven by diametrically opposed approaches to the marketplace of ideas and the nature of platforms. With regard to the latter, the Court must decide whether platforms are the equivalent of newspapers or malls. If they are a hybrid, the court must set forth clear guidelines for distinguishing the editorial function from that of closing off access to the public square. The majority sees governmental power as a threat and therefore looks to prevent the concentration of power therein. Alito approaches the marketplace of ideas from the perspective of the individual speaker. Without a strong government that can play referee between the weak and the powerful, the weaker voices will either be drowned out or edited out.[24]

One, seemingly logical, response to this situation would be to tell frustrated speakers simply to seek out another platform. This, however, ignores the concentration of media power.[25] Simply put, this approach

---

[23] *West Coast Hotel v. Parrish*, 300 U.S. 379 391 (1937).

[24] See, Fiss, supra note 15.

[25] In 2018, Of the roughly 9.5 billion "monthly active users" of social media, five platforms (Facebook, Youtube, WhatsApp, WeChat, and Instagram) accounted for roughly 7.5 billion—78.9%. See "The Rise of Social Media." https://ourworldindata.org/rise-of-social-media. 18 September 2019. Last Accessed 16 August 2024.

would compare to telling African Americans denied access to a segregated lunch counter to find another restaurant or use *The Green Book* to find an accommodation.[26] The marketplace of speech, like the marketplace of public accommodations prior to the Civil Rights Act, is not free precisely because of the absence of governmental refereeing.

NetChoice and the ensuing lower court decisions embrace much more than simple questions about the relationship between the government and the freedom of particular private actors. Instead, they raise issues concerning the role of government in playing referee in a marketplace of ideas occupied by many actors who exercise their liberties with vastly disproportionate amounts of powers. The key question is not whether a powerful government presents an Orwellian threat to powerful actors. Instead the question concerns determining an appropriate amount of power that will enable the government to prevent the establishment of a feudal cyber-marketplace of ideas that is dominated by private actors with more power than the Framers could have conceived.

---

[26] https://www.loc.gov/item/2016298176/.

CHAPTER 11

Murthy v. Missouri: Jawboning, Social Media, and the First Amendment

David L. Sloss

In *Murthy v. Missouri*,[1] two states and five social media users sued numerous federal government defendants, claiming that they coerced social media platforms to suppress protected First Amendment speech. The trial court granted a broad preliminary injunction in favor of the plaintiffs. The Fifth Circuit affirmed in part, granting a much narrower injunction, while still restricting communication between the government and social media companies.[2] The Supreme Court, in a 6–3 decision, reversed the Fifth Circuit on the grounds that none of the plaintiffs had standing to sue.

The Supreme Court noted that, for many years, Facebook and other social media platforms have taken action to suppress certain disfavored categories of speech. Suppression can take several forms. "They place warning labels on some posts, while deleting others. They also demote

[1] 144 S. Ct. 1972 (2024).
[2] Missouri v. Biden, 83 F.4th 350 (5th Cir. 2023).

D. L. Sloss (✉)
Santa Clara University Law School, Santa Clara, CA, USA
e-mail: dlsloss@scu.edu

content so that it is less visible to other users. And they may suspend or ban users who frequently post content that violates platform policies."[3] All agree that companies do not violate the First Amendment if they take such actions on their own initiative, because independent action by companies is not "state action." However, the Fifth Circuit held that government defendants likely violated the rights of social media users "by coercing and significantly encouraging social media platforms to censor disfavored speech."[4] (I say "likely" because, for the purpose of a preliminary injunction, plaintiffs simply needed to show a likelihood of success on the merits.)

Plaintiffs included the states of Missouri and Louisiana, as well as "three doctors, the owner of a news website, and a healthcare activist."[5] The initial complaint named numerous federal defendants, but the Fifth Circuit's injunction focused on five main government defendants: the White House, the Surgeon General's office, the Centers for Disease Control (CDC), the FBI, and the Cybersecurity Infrastructure Security Agency (CISA). With respect to those defendants the Fifth Circuit injunction stated (in part): "Defendants, and their employees and agents, shall take no actions, formal or informal, directly or indirectly, to coerce or significantly encourage social media companies to remove, delete, suppress, or reduce... posted social media content containing protected free speech."[6] It bears emphasis that the Fifth Circuit injunction itself censored speech by prohibiting communications between government defendants and private companies.

The Supreme Court granted cert. to consider three questions: "(1) Whether respondents have Article III standing; (2) Whether the government's challenged conduct transformed private social-media companies' content-moderation decisions into state action and violated respondents' First Amendment rights; and (3) Whether the terms and breadth of the preliminary injunction are proper."[7] The majority addressed only the first question, holding that none of the plaintiffs had standing to sue.

---

[3] *Murthy*, 144 S. Ct. at 1982.

[4] *Missouri*, 83 F.4th, at 373.

[5] *Murthy*, 144 S. Ct. at 1984.

[6] *Missouri*, 83 F.4th at 397.

[7] Murthy v. Missouri, question presented, at https://www.supremecourt.gov/qp/23-00411qp.pdf.

Justice Barrett wrote the majority opinion. She noted that federal courts may not exercise jurisdiction unless "at least one plaintiff establishes that she has standing to sue."[8] To establish standing, plaintiff must demonstrate "that she has suffered, or will suffer, an injury that is concrete, particularized, and actual or imminent; fairly traceable to the challenged action; and redressable by a favorable ruling."[9] The Court added that "a federal court cannot redress injury that results from the independent action of some third party not before the court."[10] From the Court's perspective, all of the plaintiffs lacked standing because their alleged injuries resulted from the independent actions of social media companies that were not named as defendants in the lawsuit. Plaintiffs' alleged injuries were not redressable by the courts because those companies could continue to enforce their content moderation policies against the plaintiffs, even if the Court upheld the injunction against the government defendants.

The Court divided its standing analysis into two parts. First, the Court considered "whether the plaintiffs have demonstrated traceability for their past injuries."[11] On this point, "the primary weakness in the record of past restrictions is the lack of specific causation findings with respect to any discrete instance of content moderation."[12] In other words, plaintiffs failed to identify any specific, concrete instance where a company restricted a plaintiff's speech on its platform *as a result of* government encouragement or coercion. The Court noted that "the platforms moderated similar content before any of the Government defendants engaged in the challenged conduct," and "the platforms continued to exercise their independent judgment even after communications with the defendants began."[13] Thus, most of the plaintiffs failed to show that their alleged past injuries were "fairly traceable" to the government's conduct.

The Court thought Jill Hines was in a different position than the other plaintiffs in this respect. "Of all the plaintiffs, Hines makes the

---

[8] *Murthy*, 144 S. Ct. at 1985.
[9] *Id.*, at 1986.
[10] *Id.*
[11] *Id.*, at 1987.
[12] *Id.*
[13] *Id.*

best showing of a [causal] connection between her social-media restrictions and communications between the relevant platform (Facebook) and specific defendants (CDC and the White House)."[14] Hines was a "healthcare activist" who "advocated against COVID-19 mask and vaccine mandates."[15] The Court conceded that she may have "eked out a showing of traceability for past injuries."[16]

However, "to obtain forward-looking relief, the plaintiffs must establish a substantial risk of future injury that is traceable to the Government defendants and likely to be redressed by an injunction against them."[17] Hines' claim failed in this respect because most of the government's "public and private engagement with the platforms occurred in 2021, when the pandemic was still in full swing. By August 2022, when Hines joined the case, the officials' communications about COVID-19 misinformation had slowed to a trickle."[18] Since the "frequent, intense communications that took place in 2021 had considerably subsided by 2022," the Court concluded that Hines failed to "show that she faces future harm that is traceable to officials in the White House and the Surgeon General's Office."[19] In sum, Hines failed to show a likelihood of future harm traceable to government conduct, and the other plaintiffs failed to show past harm that met the traceability (causation) requirement.

Justice Alito wrote a dissenting opinion on behalf of himself and Justices Thomas and Gorsuch. Justice Alito disagreed with the majority's standing analysis. He focused almost exclusively on Hines because she had the strongest case for standing and, under well settled principles, federal courts may exercise jurisdiction even if only one plaintiff has standing. After a lengthy analysis of the specific facts related to Hines' claim, Justice Alito concluded that "Hines met all the requirements for Article III standing."[20]

---

[14] *Id.*, at 1990.
[15] *Id.*
[16] *Id.*, at 1992.
[17] *Id.*, at 1993.
[18] *Id.*, at 1994.
[19] *Id.*
[20] *Id.*, at 2009 (Alito, J., dissenting).

Then, in his words, he proceeded to address "the merits of Hines's First Amendment claim."[21] However, Justice Alito's analysis of the merits said very little about the First Amendment. Instead, he focused almost exclusively on the question whether the speech-restrictive activities of Facebook and the other social media companies constituted "state action." That analysis turns on whether government communications with private companies crossed the line from "permissible persuasion" to "unconstitutional coercion."[22] Justice Alito concluded that the government had crossed that line, and that therefore the private companies' content moderation activities were subject to First Amendment constraints.

The majority opinion in Murthy raises but does not answer crucial questions about the application of First Amendment principles to the internet. Here, it is important to note the types of content at issue in *Murthy*. According to the government, terrorist organizations use social media platforms "as tools for recruiting, fundraising, and spreading their propaganda—including by radicalizing vulnerable individuals and inspiring attacks in the United States."[23] Additionally, "foreign governments such as Russia, China, and Iran use the platforms in influence operations that spread disinformation, sow discord, push foreign nations' policy agendas, and ultimately undermine confidence in our democratic institutions and values."[24] Additionally, much of the analysis in *Murthy* focused on coordinated efforts by the government and social media companies to limit the spread of COVID-19 misinformation that posed a risk to public health. Hence, the remainder of this analysis addresses terrorist content, foreign influence operations, and COVID-19 misinformation.

The injunction issued by the Fifth Circuit classifies all of this content as "protected free speech."[25] Indeed, the Fifth Circuit said that any "effort by administrative methods to prevent the dissemination of ideas or opinions thought dangerous or offensive… is prohibited by the First

---

[21] *Id.*
[22] *Id.*, at 2010.
[23] Murthy v. Missouri, Brief for the Petitioners, 2023 WL 8869373, at *3.
[24] *Id.*, at *4.
[25] *Missouri*, 83 F.4th at 397.

Amendment."[26] Moreover, the lower court injunction would have barred federal government employees from taking any action to "significantly encourage social-media companies to remove, delete, suppress or reduce such content."[27] Something is seriously wrong with the Court's First Amendment doctrine if it bars federal government employees from encouraging social media companies to remove or suppress terrorist recruitment material, medical misinformation that poses a threat to public health, and disinformation propagated by agents of hostile foreign states.

Justice Alito, like the Fifth Circuit, assumed without any significant analysis that the First Amendment bars the government from directly regulating the dissemination of harmful content on social media. If that assumption is correct, then it necessarily follows that the government cannot coerce social media companies to limit the spread of such content on their platforms. However, that assumption may be challenged. There is a good argument that "the Supreme Court should recognize the constitutional significance of the distinction between speech and electronic amplification of speech."[28] Electronic amplification has an expressive element, but it is primarily a commercial activity. The First Amendment specifies that "Congress shall make no law… abridging the freedom of speech." It does not say that Congress is prohibited from regulating the commercial activities of trillion-dollar companies that generate revenue by providing electronic amplification services for customers who want to disseminate their messages instantaneously to millions of people.

In light of the harm that can result from instantaneous dissemination of terrorist content and foreign propaganda to millions of recipients, the Court should arguably apply a different First Amendment analysis to the commercial activities of companies that provide electronic amplification services than it does to ordinary speech. The potential for harm in a category of speech such as support for terrorism or foreign propaganda is far greater when that speech is amplified by social media. Therefore, one could argue, the government should have greater powers to respond to those greater risks of harm. Justice Alito is correct, however, that to date the Court has not accepted this argument. Although his opinion did not

---

[26] *Id.*, at 392 n.21.

[27] *Id.*, at 397.

[28] David L. Sloss, *Stop Electronic Amplification of Lies*, 66 St. Louis Univ. L. J. 129, 146 (2021).

address tiers of scrutiny, under current First Amendment doctrine, most content-based regulation of electronic amplification services would trigger strict scrutiny.

Even if one is not persuaded by the argument that the fact of electronic amplification should alter the analysis, there are still sound reasons for courts to give the government greater leeway to regulate terrorist content, foreign propaganda, and medical misinformation than current First Amendment doctrine allows. Begin with terrorist content. In May 2019, representatives of several countries and heads of leading technology companies adopted the "Christchurch Call to Action" in response to a terrorist attack in New Zealand that was livestreamed on Facebook. Under the Christchurch Call, governments and technology companies pledged to work together "to prevent the upload of and to detect and immediately remove terrorist and violent extremist content online."[29] The United States joined the Christchurch Call in 2021.[30] However, the Supreme Court subsequently issued a decision that makes it extremely difficult, if not impossible, for civil plaintiffs to hold internet companies liable when they provide assistance for acts of international terrorism.[31] The Fifth Circuit injunction in *Murthy*, if upheld, would have interfered with the government's ability to implement its commitments under the Christchurch Call, and would make it easier for terrorists to exploit social media platforms for nefarious purposes. Although the Supreme Court decision dissolved the lower court injunction, it did not resolve the primary constitutional question: does the First Amendment prevent the federal government from "significantly encouraging" (as opposed to coercing) social media companies to block or remove terrorist content? The answer should be a resounding "No,"[32] but this remains an open question under current doctrine.

Next, consider foreign influence operations. Agents of Russia, China, Iran, and North Korea, among others, are presently engaged in global

---

[29] The Christchurch Call Commitments, at https://www.christchurchcall.org/the-christchurch-call-commitments/ (visited July 19, 2024).

[30] Department of State, Press Statement (May 7, 2021), at https://www.state.gov/united-states-joins-christchurch-call-to-action-to-eliminate-terrorist-and-violent-extremist-content-online/.

[31] *See* Twitter, Inc. v. Taamneh, 598 U.S. 471 (2023).

[32] *See* David L. Sloss, *Civil Liability for Internet Companies to Help Prevent International Terrorism* (Transnational Litigation Blog, June 6, 2023).

efforts to subvert democracy and bolster authoritarian governance. They exploit social media platforms, such as Facebook and YouTube, as "weapons" in their ongoing campaign of information warfare.[33] After revelations emerged about Russian interference in the 2016 U.S. Presidential election,[34] the major social media companies invested significant resources in their efforts to combat election interference and online disinformation. More recently, though, "faced with economic headwinds and political and legal pressure, the social media giants have shown signs that fighting false information online is no longer as high a priority."[35] Consequently, "we now have less information than ever before about the impact our underregulated social media platforms are having on our politics."[36] The Fifth Circuit injunction in *Murthy*, if upheld, would have exacerbated this problem by inhibiting government efforts to collaborate with internet companies to combat Chinese and Russian information warfare. Thanks to the Supreme Court decision, we dodged that bullet temporarily, but the underlying problem remains. Current First Amendment doctrine creates an obstacle that makes it difficult for the federal government to perform one of its most vital missions: protecting American democracy from the threat of information warfare.

Finally, consider the case of COVID-19 misinformation. *Murthy* raises the following question: In the midst of a global pandemic that killed more than one million Americans and more than seven million people worldwide, can we trust government experts to make informed, reasoned decisions about what medical information is false, and about which false information poses a danger to public health? In *United States v. Alvarez*,[37] Justice Alito wrote a powerful dissent in which he argued that "the right to free speech does not protect false factual statements that inflict real harm and serve no legitimate interest."[38] In *Murthy*, the government

---

[33] *See* David L. Sloss, *Tyrants on Twitter: Protecting Democracies from Information Warfare* (2022).

[34] *See* Kathleen Hall Jamieson, *Cyber-War: How Russian Hackers and Trolls Helped Elect a President* (2018).

[35] Steven Lee Myers and Nico Grant, *Combating Disinformation Wanes at Social Media Giants* (New York Times, Feb. 14, 2023).

[36] Julia Angwin, *Why the False Narratives About Trump are Likely to Spread* (New York Times, July 16, 2024).

[37] 567 U.S. 709 (2012).

[38] *Id.*, at 739 (Alito, J., dissenting).

claimed that it was trying to prevent social media companies from disseminating false factual statements about COVID that inflicted real harm and served no legitimate interest. Justice Alito's dissenting opinion in *Murthy* makes clear that he does not trust government officials to make expert decisions as to what medical misinformation presents a serious danger to public health.[39]

But if we cannot trust the government's public health experts to make these types of decisions, who can we trust? Facebook and Google do not have the in-house expertise to determine for themselves whether factual statements about COVID are true or false, nor do they have the expertise to decide which false claims pose a serious danger to public health. Federal judges also lack the technical expertise to make such decisions, as do members of the general public who are social media users. Many American citizens do not trust government experts, and much of modern First Amendment doctrine is founded on the premise that "the Constitution protects speech... because the government is so dangerous in its capacity to abuse its regulatory power."[40] Ultimately, *Murthy* leaves unanswered one of the central questions of First Amendment law in the age of social media: in what circumstances can we (or should we) trust government experts to decide what content on social media platforms is both false and dangerous? The Supreme Court has not yet seriously grappled with this question.

---

[39] *See Murthy*, 144 S. Ct. at 1997–2015 (Alito, J., dissenting).

[40] Helen Norton, *Distrust, Negative First Amendment Theory, and the Regulation of Lies*, 4 J. Free Speech Law 595, 596–97 (2023).

CHAPTER 12

NRA v. Vullo: On the Line Between Government Persuasion and Government Coercion

Paul E. McGreal

When government officials speak to the public, the First Amendment takes a mostly hands-off approach. Officials may promote a particular viewpoint with no obligation to give equal support to another.[1] Officials can also criticize viewpoints they disagree with, even using strong language, and the Free Speech Clause will not stop them. That is, until their words cross the line from persuasion to coercion. While government officials may do their best to convince the public, they cannot make threats to silence speakers they disagree with.

National Rifle Association v. Vullo was about drawing the line between persuasion and coercion. At the time of the 2018 school shooting in Parkland, Florida, New York State officials spoke out against gun violence and what they saw as irresponsible behavior by the National Rifle Association

---

[1] Rust v. Sullivan, 500 U.S. 173, 193 (1991).

P. E. McGreal (✉)
Creighton University School of Law, Omaha, NE, USA
e-mail: paulmcgreal@creighton.edu

(NRA). The Free Speech Clause protects such public advocacy. The NRA, however, claimed that the state officials went further. In speaking with the insurance companies they regulated, the officials allegedly threatened legal action if the companies did not sever all ties with the NRA. Those threats, if proven, would violate the First Amendment.

Bantam Books and the Persuasion-Coercion Distinction

The Supreme Court's prior cases had made two points crystal clear. On the one hand, "[a] government official can share her views freely and criticize particular beliefs, and she can do so forcefully in the hopes of persuading others to follow her lead." On the other hand, the Free Speech Clause prohibits a government official from "us[ing] the power of the State to punish or suppress disfavored expression."[2] It is easy to see that the government is punishing or suppressing speech when a law directly stops someone from speaking, like when an ordinance prohibits homeowners from displaying yard signs on their property. The question is more difficult when the government is accused of indirectly censoring speech by pressuring a private person to punish a speaker. In that case, the government is arguably trying to circumvent the First Amendment by doing indirectly what it cannot do directly.

The Court first addressed indirect punishment of speech in the 1963 case *Bantam.Books, Inc. v. Sullivan*.[3] That case involved a Rhode Island state commission that advised state officials about the enforcement of a state law that banned the sale of obscene printed materials. The commission allegedly targeted four New York publishers whose books the commission members found objectionable. Because the publishers operated outside of Rhode Island, the commission could not directly punish them for publishing the books. Instead, the commission went after the Rhode Island book distributor that purchased and re-sold the books. The New York publishers claimed that the commission had harassed and intimidated the distributor to get it to stop buying the publishers' books. When the distributor gave in, the publishers sued the commission for violating the First Amendment.

---

[2] NRA v. Vullo, 602 U.S. 175, 188 (2024).
[3] 372 U.S. 58 (1963).

The Court focused on whether the commission had indirectly censored the New York publishers by putting pressure on the distributor. The commission was only advisory, so it did not have the power to prosecute a private business like the distributor. The commission, however, could take other actions that might lead to a prosecution. For example, it could send official notices to distributors that listed books the commission found offensive, recommend that the state attorney general prosecute a distributor, and notify police departments of businesses that sold offensive materials. In the *Bantam Books* case, the commission's notices not only identified books from the New York publishers that the distributor should stop selling, but also "thanked" the distributor for its expected "cooperation" and explained that the commission could recommend legal action against businesses that did not comply. Not surprisingly, the distributor stopped purchasing books from the New York publishers, even ones that did not violate Rhode Island law.[4]

When the book publishers sued the commission, the commission argued that it did nothing to punish the publishers directly: any harm came from the distributor's independent decision to stop purchasing their books. The Court disagreed, deciding that the commission had "coerced" the distributor to drop the publishers' books. The commission's notices and collaboration with local police departments, along with its power to recommend legal actions, were a looming threat to anyone who continued to sell the objectionable books. Heeding that threat, the distributor stopped purchasing the books. Thus, by coercing the distributor, the commission suppressed the publisher's speech in violation of the First Amendment.[5]

Bantam Books applied an important First Amendment rule—government officials violate the Free Speech Clause when they coerce someone to punish or suppress speech that the government officials do not like. Coercion occurs when a person reasonably believes that officials are threatening them with punishment unless they take action, like discontinuing book purchases. To bring this type of legal claim, the NRA would have to show that New York state officials coerced someone, like the insurance companies, to punish the NRA because the officials disagreed with its gun rights advocacy.

---

[4] *Id.* at 63.
[5] *Id.* at 71–72.

A Word About Procedure and the "Facts" of the Case

To fully understand *NRA v. Vullo*, we need a brief detour into court procedure. The NRA filed a lawsuit in federal court against three defendants: the New York State Department of Financial Services, which is the state agency that regulates insurance companies; the Department's former superintendent, Maria Vullo; and former New York Governor Andrew Cuomo. To begin the lawsuit, the NRA filed a document that did two things: first, it provided a factual narrative of what the NRA claimed that the defendants did and said, and second, it explained why the NRA believed that the defendants had violated the Free Speech Clause. In response, Vullo filed a motion to dismiss that made a very narrow legal argument: *even if* all of the facts in the NRA's complaint were true, those facts did not show that the defendants had violated the Free Speech Clause. Vullo did not concede that the NRA's facts were true, but only assumed they were true for purposes of making a legal argument. A defendant will make this type of motion to try to end a lawsuit before spending time and money investigating and proving the actual facts of the case. Thus, when *NRA v. Vullo* arrived at the Supreme Court, we only had the NRA's version of what happened.[6] To defeat a motion to dismiss, the NRA only needed to convince a court that its version of the facts stated a plausible legal claim. Recall that under the *Bantam Books* case, the NRA's legal claim would be that the defendants had coerced insurance companies to stop doing business with the NRA because of its gun rights advocacy. And coercion would have occurred if the insurance companies reasonably understood the defendants to threaten enforcement action unless the companies cut ties with the NRA. The question in *NRA v. Vullo*, then, was whether the NRA's version of the facts made it plausible that the insurance companies reasonably felt threatened by the defendants.

---

[6] Documents filed in the case can be found on SCOTUSblog at the following link: https://www.scotusblog.com/case-files/cases/national-rifle-association-of-america-v-vullo/ (last visited August 11, 2024).

Justice Sotomayor's Opinion for the Court

The NRA claimed the Vullo objected to its speech advocating for the rights of gun owners. As head of a government agency that regulates insurance, Vullo did not have legal authority to directly restrict the NRA's speech. Vullo did, however, have power over the insurance companies that did business with the NRA. The NRA claimed that Vullo used that power to pressure insurance companies to do what she couldn't—punish the NRA for its speech. And that's exactly what the NRA claimed had happened—the insurance companies cut ties with the NRA, which caused substantial economic harm.

Under the *Bantam Books* case, the question was whether Vullo had coerced the insurance companies to stop working with the NRA. And coercion depended on whether the insurance companies would reasonably understand Vullo's actions or words as threatening legal action if they did not cut ties with the NRA. The case turned on this key question.

To answer the question, Justice Sotomayor's opinion focused on two points: first, Vullo's authority as head of the Department; and, second, what Vullo did and said when working with the insurance companies. As to the question Vullo's authority, Vullo had greater power than the commission in the *Bantam Books* case. While the commission could only recommend actions against distributors, Vullo could actually take legal action against insurance companies. Vullo, then, could directly carry out any threats she made to the insurance companies.

Against the background of this power, Vullo's alleged words and actions could lead the insurance companies to reasonably believe that they would be punished unless they cut ties with the NRA. Vullo first contacted the insurance companies about so-called "affinity" insurance policies they had collaborated with the NRA to offer its members. Insurance companies work with universities, associations, and other groups to offer such policies as a special benefit to their members. Vullo notified the insurance companies that aspects of the NRA affinity policies violated state insurance laws, and that the Department could take legal action if those policies continued. At this point, there was no coercion—Vullo had simply communicated with a regulated company about its compliance with state law.

However, as Vullo continued communicating with the insurance companies, the threat came into view. To start, the companies had affinity insurance policies with many organizations, yet Vullo focused her warnings on the NRA. In addition, Vullo said that the Department would overlook legal issues with the other affinity policies if the insurance companies dropped *all* insurance policies with the NRA, including general corporate liability policies that were perfectly legal. Vullo then followed up on these conversations with official written communications that repeated the legal concerns with the NRA's affinity insurance policies. The insurance companies got the message—if you want to avoid legal action, cut all ties with the NRA.

The larger political and social context explained *why* Vullo allegedly pressured the insurance companies to target the NRA. Around that time, a shooter at the Marjory Stoneman Douglas High School in Parkland, Florida, killed 17 students, teachers, and staff. After the shooting, Vullo and other state officials spoke out against gun violence and strongly criticized what they saw as the NRA's role in school shootings. This background provided a plausible motive for Vullo's threat to the insurance companies—punishing the NRA for its gun rights advocacy.

Based on all of these facts, the Court decided that the NRA had had offered a plausible story that "Vullo violated the First Amendment by coercing [the insurance companies] to terminate their business relationships with the NRA to punish or suppress the NRA's advocacy." Coercion was plausible because Vullo allegedly singled out the NRA and urged the insurance companies to take action or suffer the legal consequences.

The Concurring Opinions

Justices Neil Gorsuch and Ketanji Brown Jackson wrote concurring opinions that clarified why they agreed with the Court's decision. Justice Gorsuch emphasized that the critical question in a case like this is whether a government official coerced a private party to punish someone else's speech. Whether coercion exists in any particular case will depend on all the facts and circumstances of the situation. Thus, trial courts should not focus on any single fact or factor, like whether the government official had enforcement authority.

Justice Jackson's opinion emphasized a key point about the meaning of the Free Speech Clause. A government official does not violate that Clause simply by coercing a private party, like the insurance companies. Rather, the private party must be coerced to do something that violates the Free Speech Clause. For example, it would *not* have violated the

Free Speech Clause if all Vullo did was coerce the insurance companies to discontinue the illegal affinity insurance policies. That would have been legitimate law enforcement. It would violate the Free Speech Clause, however, to coerce the insurance companies to retaliate against the NRA's gun rights speech by cutting *all* ties with the NRA. Justice Jackson clarified the type of coercion required to state a legal claim under the First Amendment.

Unfinished Business and Lessons Learned

The Court's decision in *NRA v. Vullo* leaves unfinished business for the legal case, with the lawsuit returning to the federal trial court for further proceedings. Unless the parties settle, they will start investigating the facts in a process known as "discovery," where they question witnesses, review documents, and collect evidence. Depending on how discovery goes, the case may go to trial, where a jury would decide whose version of the facts they believe. So, even though Vullo lost the motion to dismiss, she could still win the lawsuit, depending on the evidence and what a jury decides.

Government officials would be wise to take two lessons from *NRA v. Vullo*. First, if they focus enforcement efforts on a single organization, they should have a reason unrelated to its public advocacy. The NRA alleged that Vullo had no legitimate reason to single it out when other organizations also had affinity insurance programs that violated state law. This made it plausible that Vullo had retaliated against the NRA for its gun rights advocacy. The case would have been different if the NRA's insurance plans were particularly problematic under state insurance law, perhaps because they involved predatory marketing or terms. After *NRA v. Vullo*, government officials should ask whether they have a good reason for targeting an organization for legal action.

Second, when communicating with regulated companies, government officials should not comment about discontinuing *lawful* business with other companies. While Vullo had good reason to urge insurance companies to discontinue the illegal affinity insurance programs with the NRA, she had no legitimate reason to suggest that they stop doing lawful business with the NRA. Consequently, it appeared that Vullo simply wanted to punish the NRA for its gun rights advocacy. Going forward, government officials should limit law enforcement threats to activities that arguably violate the law.

CHAPTER 13

Lindke v. Freed & *O'Connor-Radcliff v. Garnier*: State Action & the First Amendment

Eric T. Kasper

Social media has become an integral part of many people's lives. On Facebook, Instagram, Snapchat, TikTok, and X (formerly known as Twitter), millions of Americans log on every day to find news, comment on issues, and publish information about their lives. These platforms have become, as the Supreme Court opined in *Packingham v. North Carolina* (2017), "the most important places (in a spatial sense) for the exchange of views" today, as they are "the modern public square."[1] This is also true for public officials, who might use social media for many purposes, including communicating with constituents, appealing to voters, and sharing personal content with family and friends. When a public official deletes another user's comments from that official's social media page or blocks a user's account entirely, does it violate the First Amendment? This

[1] 582 U.S. 98, 104, 107 (2017).

E. T. Kasper (✉)
University of Wisconsin-Eau Claire, Eau Claire, WI, USA
e-mail: kasperet@uwec.edu

was at issue in *Lindke v. Freed* and *O'Connor-Radcliff v. Garnier*. The answer lies, in part, in whether the public official was engaged in state action when preventing someone from posting on that official's page.

The Legal Context

Under the First Amendment, speech has its highest level of protection in traditional public forums, which include streets and parks.[2] If the government imposes a content-based restriction on speech in a traditional public forum, "it must show that its regulation is necessary to serve a compelling state interest and that it is narrowly drawn to achieve that end."[3] That same test is required if the government designates a public forum, meaning it opens a forum for speech when it is not required to do so, such as with public university meeting facilities or an open forum during a school board meeting.[4] This test is known as strict scrutiny, and it has been characterized as "'strict' in theory and fatal in fact,"[5] although the "fatal" nature of the test has been called into question in recent years.[6] Nevertheless, it remains a demanding standard, which the government rarely meets, making content-based exclusions on speech in public forums likely to be found unconstitutional.[7] Importantly, in *Packingham* the Supreme Court applied the same scrutiny to government restrictions on social media users' expression as it does to government restrictions on speech in more traditional spatial forums.[8] The Supreme Court's

---

[2] Hague v. Comm. for Indus. Org., 307 U.S. 496, 515 (1939).

[3] Perry Educ. Ass'n v. Perry Loc. Educators' Ass'n, 460 U.S. 37, 45 (1983).

[4] *Perry*, 460 U.S. at 45–46.

[5] Gerald Gunther, "The Supreme Court, 1971 Term—Forward: In Search of Evolving Doctrine on a Changing Court: A Model for a Newer Equal Protection," 86 *Harvard Law Review* 1, 8 (1972).

[6] *See* Adam Winkler, "Fatal in Theory and Strict in Fact: An Empirical Analysis of Strict Scrutiny in the Federal Courts," 59 *Vanderbilt Law Review* 793 (2006); Matthew D. Bunker, Clay Calvert, and William C. Nevin, "Strict in Theory, But Feeble in Fact?: First Amendment Strict Scrutiny and the Protection of Speech," 16 *Communication Law and Policy* 349 (2011).

[7] Content neutral government restrictions on speech in public forums are subject to the less demanding standard of intermediate scrutiny. *Packingham*, 582 U.S. at 105.

[8] *Packingham*, 582 U.S. at 104.

ruling in *Packingham* did *not* declare that social media platforms themselves are public forums under the First Amendment, and more recently the Supreme Court has clarified that, as a general matter, social media platforms are private entities with their own First Amendment rights to restrict who may speak on their websites.[9] Rather, in *Packingham* the Supreme Court, in reviewing a government policy prohibiting certain users from accessing social media, applied the same scrutiny to that prohibition as it applies to government restrictions on the time, place, and manner of expression in traditional public forums.[10]

But these First Amendment rules are relevant only if the government has acted. Usually, there is no question about this, as a lawsuit challenging unconstitutional conduct is filed against a government entity clearly acting in an official capacity, such as with action by a police officer on duty, or when the government restricts speech by passing a law (as was the case in *Packingham*). But sometimes the question is more complicated, as it may not be clear if the entity regulating speech is acting on behalf of the government. This distinction is important because, the Supreme Court has held that "the Free Speech Clause prohibits only *governmental* abridgment of speech. The Free Speech Clause does not prohibit *private* abridgment of speech."[11] A private actor has their own First Amendment rights, and they may choose not to host someone else's speech. If a private business removes a speaker from its property, the First Amendment typically would not provide any protection to that speaker. Nevertheless, under a narrow set of conditions, an otherwise private entity could be acting "under color of law," meaning it engages in "state action," which the Supreme Court has held includes when one's actions are "fairly attributable to the State."[12] For public employees, the Supreme Court held that "generally, a public employee acts under color of state law while acting in his official capacity or while exercising his responsibilities

---

[9] *See* Moody v. NetChoice, LLC, 144 S. Ct. 2383, 2394 (2024) ("this Court has many times held, in many contexts, that it is no job for government to decide what counts as the right balance of private expression—to 'un-bias' what it thinks biased, rather than to leave such judgments to speakers and their audiences. That principle works for social-media platforms as it does for others.").

[10] *Packingham*, 582 U.S. at 105–08.

[11] Manhattan Community Access Corp. v. Halleck, 587 U.S. 802, 808 (2019) (emphasis in original).

[12] Lugar v. Edmondson Oil Co., 457 U.S. 922, 937 (1982).

pursuant to state law."[13] State action is required to file a federal lawsuit under federal law (42 U.S.C. § 1983) when alleging unconstitutional action.

The Facts of *Lindke* and *O'Connor-Radcliff*

In *Lindke v. Freed*, James Freed opened a private Facebook account while he was a college student. As his popularity grew online and he approached having 5000 Facebook "friends" (the limit of the number of friends a user can have), he changed his profile to public, allowing anyone to see his posts and make their own comments on them. In 2014, Freed became the city manager of Port Huron, Michigan, and he updated his Facebook page: he added his job title, linked to the city's website, and posted a photo of himself wearing a city lapel pin. He continued operating his page himself and posting personal content, including about his family and religious beliefs. Freed also posted information about Port Huron, including city activities, press releases, and reports. Freed asked for public feedback, and Facebook users often commented on his posts, with Freed frequently replying to comments.

During the COVID-19 pandemic, Freed made personal posts about being with his family at home and outside. He also posted city-related information, such as a hiring freeze and a press release about a relief package. Kevin Lindke made comments on Freed's Facebook page, critiquing the city's pandemic response as "abysmal," and complaining that "the city deserves better."[14] After Freed posted a picture of himself and the mayor picking up a takeout meal, Lindke commented that "residents are suffering," while politicians were dining out, "instead of talking to the community."[15] Freed first deleted Lindke's comments and later blocked him. After Lindke was blocked, he could view Freed's posts but could not comment on them. Lindke filed a lawsuit alleging that Freed had violated his First Amendment rights, claiming that Freed, as a government official, had created a public forum with his Facebook page. A U.S. district court and the Sixth Circuit found for Freed. Both courts charactered Freed's Facebook page as a private activity, making

---

[13] West v. Atkins, 487 U.S. 42, 50 (1988).
[14] Lindke v. Freed, 601 U.S. 187, 193 (2024).
[15] *Lindke*, 601 U.S. at 193.

the First Amendment inapplicable. The Sixth Circuit's test for whether a public official's social media activity is state action asked, "if the 'text of state law requires an officeholder to maintain a social-media account,' the official 'use[s]...state resources' or 'government staff' to run the account, or the 'accoun[t] belong[s] to an office, rather than an individual officeholder.'".[16]

O'Connor-Radcliff v. Garnier was a companion case to *Lindke*. Michelle O'Connor-Radcliff and T.J. Zane were two candidates running for the Poway Unified School District Board of Trustees in California. O'Connor-Radcliff and Zane each had personal Facebook pages, but for their respective campaigns they each created public Facebook pages. On these public pages, O'Connor-Radcliff and Zane campaigned and posted information about issues relevant to the school district. After they won their respective elections, O'Connor-Radcliff and Zane each continued using their public pages to post information about the school board, including about budgeting, board meetings, and public safety. O'Connor-Radcliff and Zane's pages each designated that they were a "government official." O'Connor-Radcliff operated a similar Twitter page.

Christopher and Kimberly Garnier are parents of children attending the Poway Unified School District. They made what the Supreme Court characterized as "lengthy and repetitive" criticisms of O'Connor-Radcliff and Zane on social media. This included nearly identical comments on 42 of O'Connor-Radcliff's Facebook posts and 226 identical replies to O'Connor-Radcliff's tweets. O'Connor-Radcliff and Zane deleted the Garniers' comments before eventually blocking them. The Garniers filed a lawsuit alleging First Amendment violations. A U.S. district court and the Ninth Circuit ruled that O'Connor-Radcliff and Zane were acting "under color of law" on their public social media pages, allowing the lawsuit to proceed. The Ninth Circuit's test to reach this conclusion was as follows: "an off-duty state employee acts under color of law if she (1) 'purports to or pretends to act under color of law'; (2) her 'pretense of acting in the performance of [her] duties had the purpose and effect of influencing the behavior of others'; and (3) the 'harm inflicted on plaintiff related in some meaningful way either to the officer's governmental status or to the

---

[16] *Lindke*, 601 U.S. at 194 (quoting Lindke v. Freed, 37 F.4th 1199, 1203–04 [6th Cir. 2022]).

performance of [her] duties.'"[17] Since the Sixth Circuit and the Ninth Circuit used different tests to determine if a public official's social media activity constitutes state action, the Supreme Court granted certiorari.

SUPREME COURT RULINGS IN *Lindke* AND *O'Connor-Radcliff*

If the public officials in these cases deleted users' posts and blocked them in their capacities as state actors, there would be a plausible claim that they engaged in content discrimination, triggering First Amendment scrutiny. But were they engaged in state action? In a unanimous opinion by Justice Amy Coney Barrett, the Supreme Court clarified in *Lindke* that public officials are not "always on the clock," because they "are also private citizens with their own constitutional rights," including First Amendment rights.[18] The Supreme Court reasoned that "if Freed acted in his private capacity when he blocked Lindke and deleted his comments, he did not violate Lindke's First Amendment rights—instead, he exercised his own."[19]

When is a government official engaged in state action on social media? The Supreme Court in *Lindke* said that this requires examining the facts under a two-prong test that differed slightly from both appellate courts below: when a government official posts on social media, it is state action "only if the official (1) possessed actual authority to speak on the State's behalf, and (2) purported to exercise that authority when he spoke on social media."[20]

The first prong of *Lindke* reflects that state action must be "traceable to the State's power or authority," because "[p]rivate action—no matter how 'official' it looks—lacks the necessary lineage."[21] An official *appearing* to have a government social media page is not enough to make it state action; instead, the official must be entrusted with relevant government power to act. This power can come from written law (a

---

[17] O'Connor-Ratcliff v. Garnier, 601 U.S. 205, 207–08 (2024) (quoting Garnier v. O'Connor-Ratcliff, 41 F.4th 1158, 1170 [9th Cir. 2022]).

[18] *Lindke*, 601 U.S. at 196.

[19] *Lindke*, 601 U.S. at 197.

[20] *Lindke*, 601 U.S. at 198.

[21] *Lindke*, 601 U.S. at 198.

statute, ordinance, or regulation), or it can come from custom or usage—such as when previous holders of that office used official social media pages long enough to make the practice "permanent and well settled."[22] The Supreme Court cautioned, though, that this activity must "*actually* [be] part of the job that the State entrusted the official to do," and cannot be accomplished by the government writing "excessively broad job descriptions."[23]

Lindke's second prong explains that state action only occurs when an official uses state authority. An official would need to "use his speech in furtherance of his official responsibilities" for it to be state action.[24] To demonstrate this, the Supreme Court posed a hypothetical: a school board president making an announcement at a board meeting about school regulations is state action in an official capacity, but the same statement by that board president at a backyard barbeque to friends with children in the school district is private action in a personal capacity. For social media, one way to distinguish between these two scenarios is for the page to explicitly state what type of account it is. If the account states it is a "personal" page, without strong evidence to the contrary, "we can safely presume that speech…is personal."[25] But if the social media account "belongs to a political subdivision…or is passed down to whomever occupies a particular office," then it speaks for the government.[26]

In *Lindke*, the Supreme Court declined to rule if Freed engaged in state action when deleting Lindke's comments and blocking him. The Supreme Court remanded the case for the lower courts to determine if Freed had authority to speak for the government and if his Facebook page was official or personal, as the Supreme Court surmised, it could be a "mixed use" account with both personal and official elements.[27] In a short per curiam opinion in *O'Connor-Radcliff*, the Supreme Court

---

[22] *Lindke*, 601 U.S. at 200 (quoting Adickes v. S. H. Kress & Co., 398 U.S. 144, 168 [1970]).

[23] *Lindke*, 601 U.S. at 201 (emphasis in original).

[24] *Lindke*, 601 U.S. at 201.

[25] *Lindke*, 601 U.S. at 202.

[26] *Lindke*, 601 U.S. at 202.

[27] *Lindke*, 601 U.S. at 201–03.

similarly vacated the lower court's ruling and remanded it for lower courts to apply the *Lindke* standard.[28]

Implications for the Future

The Supreme Court understood the wide-reaching effects of its *Lindke* decision, noting there "are approximately 20 million state and local government employees across the Nation, with an extraordinarily wide range of job descriptions—from Governors, mayors, and police chiefs to teachers, healthcare professionals, and transportation workers."[29] It would behoove officials who use social media to review their accounts and practices for the factors the Supreme Court said were relevant in *Lindke*.

This begins with clarifying if a public employee possesses government authority to operate an official social media account that can be deemed a public forum with First Amendment protections for users who comment on that page. Government offices should review job descriptions and written legal requirements for any language mandating if an officeholder must operate a social media account. Similarly, if an official takes charge of an account operated by their predecessor in that position, activity by the official on that account would almost certainly be state action. Conversely, if a government official wants to clarify that their social media account is private (where they are exercising their own First Amendment rights), they should explicitly state that it is a personal account and ensure it is not managed by a government employee under their supervision.

Finally, the Supreme Court in *Lindke* provided a warning about social media actions that can carry greater liability, particularly if one operates an official or "mixed use" account. If an official deletes another user's comments, the only posts relevant to the question of whether state action occurred are those where the comments are removed. On the other hand, if an official blocks another user, then the question of state action would apply to any posts the official made on that account where the blocked user could have commented without being blocked.[30] Thus, unless it is unambiguously clear that the official is operating a private account, an official should only delete user comments with caution, and they should

---

[28] *O'Connor-Ratcliff*, 601 U.S. at 208.

[29] *Lindke*, 601 U.S. at 197.

[30] *See Lindke*, 601 U.S. at 204.

only block other users with *extreme* caution. Otherwise, it risks being state action that violates the First Amendment rights of the users who can no longer speak in an online forum created by a government official.

CHAPTER 14

United States v. Rahimi: Setting Limits on the "Right to Bear Arms"

Doni Gewirtzman

United States v. Rahimi represents the Court's first concerted effort to address a critical unresolved question about the Second Amendment's right to bear arms: under what circumstances can the government disarm a person it believes to be dangerous? In an 8–1 decision written by Chief Justice Roberts, the Court upheld a federal statute that prohibits persons who are subject to domestic violence restraining orders from possessing a firearm. While the outcome was seen as a victory for gun control advocates, the decision itself is fairly narrow in scope, leaving several important questions about the Second Amendment unresolved. And, despite the eight-justice majority, the case produced five concurring opinions and a single dissent, suggesting some ongoing tension among the justices about the future direction of Second Amendment doctrine.

D. Gewirtzman (✉)
New York Law School, West Broadway, New York, NY, USA
e-mail: doni.gewirtzman@nyls.edu

© The Author(s), under exclusive license to Springer Nature Switzerland AG 2025
H. Schweber (ed.), *SCOTUS 2024*,
https://doi.org/10.1007/978-3-031-78551-1_14

Background

Rahimi arrived at the Court against the backdrop of two modern Second Amendment precedents that transformed the constitutional status of gun rights: *District of Columbia v. Heller*[1] and *New York State Rifle & Pistol Association v. Bruen*.[2] In *Heller*, the Court held for the first time that the Second Amendment protects an individual right to possess a handgun in the home for self-defense purposes. Notably, *Heller* described the individual right as belonging to "law-abiding" and "responsible" citizens,[3] and specifically stated that the decision should not disrupt existing laws restricting firearm possession by convicted felons.[4]

In 2022, 14 years after *Heller*, the Court decided to revisit the Second Amendment in *Bruen*, a challenge to a New York statute requiring a permit to carry a handgun in public. In striking down the law, Justice Clarence Thomas' majority opinion broadly embraced originalism by instructing lower courts to engage in a two-step approach to gun regulations subject to Second Amendment challenges. Under Step One, a court must first assess whether a gun regulation violates the "plain text" of the Second Amendment. Then, under Step Two, the government bears the burden of showing that its regulation is consistent with the nation's "historical tradition" of firearm regulation.[5] In practice, this has required the government to identify analogous firearm restrictions that were in place at or around the time of the Founding.

Bruen is, arguably, the most originalist opinion ever issued by the Supreme Court. In order to interpret and apply the Second Amendment, *Bruen* charged lower court judges with the task of going back in time and reviewing historical precedents from English common law, colonial law, and early American law from the eighteenth and nineteenth centuries to determine the existence and scope of a "historical tradition," and then to assess whether a contemporary gun control regulation fell within that tradition. Rather than invoking the standard constitutional rights methodology, which focuses on the government's reasons

---

[1] 554 U.S. 570 (2008).
[2] 597 U.S. 1 (2022).
[3] *Heller*, 554 U.S. at 635.
[4] *Heller*, 554 U.S. at 626.
[5] *Bruen*, at 17.

for adopting a regulation (including the need to address the very real problem of gun violence) and the means the government is using to accomplish those goals, *Bruen* turned Second Amendment litigation into a battle of historical analogues, with each side pointing to the presence (or lack) of Founding era firearms regulations to make its case.

Bruen had an immediate impact on the outcome of Second Amendment challenges in the lower courts. Within one year of the decision, *Bruen* tilted the balance strongly in favor of litigants bringing constitutional challenges to gun restrictions, who began to win their cases at a much higher rate when compared with the 14-year interregnum between *Heller* and *Bruen*.[6]

Bruen also caused confusion and pushback from lower court judges, who struggled with how to apply the "historical tradition" standard in practice. Among other things, it was unclear how to determine whether a historical analogue was "relevantly similar," which historical periods courts should consult to locate a "historical tradition," the relevance of non-statutory historical sources, and whether judges have the institutional competence to assess and review historical data. *Bruen* also left lower court judges with a "level of abstraction" problem: how precise a historical analogue does the government have to offer in order to meet its burden of proof? Does the historical gun regulation have to be an identical match for the regulation under review, or is it sufficient to identify historical gun regulations that are motivated by similar concerns? The result was repeated calls from lower court judges for greater clarity and guidance from the Supreme Court about how to implement *Bruen*.[7]

Given this context, when the Court granted cert in *Rahimi*, there was some hope that the justices would use the case as an opportunity to clarify (a) how exactly lower courts should apply *Bruen*'s historical tradition standard, and (b) the extent to which Second Amendment allows the government to disarm dangerous persons. As it turned out, the Court left a definitive resolution of these questions for another day.

---

[6] Jacob D. Charles, *The Dead Hand of the Silent Past: Bruen, Gun Rights, and the Shackles of History*, 73 Duke L.J. 67, 122–128 (2023).

[7] *United States v. Rahimi*, 602 U.S. __, slip op. at 2–3 n.1 (Jackson, J., concurring).

The Case

There is little question that the defendant in the case, Zackey Rahimi, is a dangerous man. In December 2019, Rahimi violently assaulted his girlfriend C.M. in a parking lot. Rahimi then pulled a gun out of his car and fired shots in the direction of his fleeing girlfriend, and later threatened to shoot C.M. if she reported the incident. Shortly thereafter, a Texas state court concluded that Rahimi posed a credible threat to C.M.'s physical safety and entered a restraining order prohibiting Rahimi from threatening or contacting C.M. for two years. The order also suspected Rahimi's gun license.

Rahimi then violated the terms of his restraining order by repeatedly attempting to contact C.M. and threatening a different woman with a gun. Subsequently, the police identified Rahimi as a suspect in at least five additional shootings and searched his residence, where they discovered a pistol, a rifle, ammunition, and a copy of his restraining order.

Federal prosecutors then indicted Rahimi for violating 18 U.S.C. §922(g)(8), a federal statute that prohibits subjects of domestic violence restraining orders from possessing a firearm. Rahimi moved to dismiss the indictment, arguing that the statute violated his Second Amendment right to bear arms.

After a District Court judge rejected the challenge, the Fifth Circuit Court of Appeals reversed, holding that the federal statute violated the Second Amendment. The appellate court relied heavily on *Bruen*, concluding that §922(g)(8) fell outside the nation's "historical tradition" of gun regulation because the government failed to identify a suitable historical analogue. The government's case was hampered, of course, by the fact that domestic violence restraining orders simply did not exist during the Founding era. As a result, the government's relied on other historical regulations that disarmed other groups of citizens who were not "law abiding" or "responsible." The Fifth Circuit dismissed those historical analogues as distinguishable, held statute was facially unconstitutional (meaning it could not be constitutionally applied to anyone, including persons who were not parties to the case), and vacated Rahimi's conviction.

The Majority Opinion

In overturning the lower court ruling and rejecting Rahimi's Second Amendment challenge, Chief Justice Roberts' majority opinion held the Fifth Circuit misapplied *Bruen* by requiring the government to identify a "historical twin" to the federal statute. The Chief Justice noted that *Bruen* was "not meant to suggest a law trapped in amber,"[8] and "the Second Amendment permits more than just those regulations found identical to ones that could be found in 1791."[9]

In place of a "historical twin," Roberts directed lower courts to focus their historical tradition inquiry at a slightly higher level of abstraction, referring to larger "*principles* that underpin our regulatory tradition" when determining whether a historical analogue is "relevantly similar."[10] The shift from "historical twins" to "principles" made all the difference for the government's case. Despite the lack of any Founding era laws that specifically addressed individuals subject to domestic violence restraining orders, the Court cited restrictions from English common law and eighteenth-century state laws that effectively disarmed persons the state believed presented "a clear threat of physical violence to another."[11] It recognized that §922(g)(8) was "by no means identical to these founding era regimes, but it does not need to be" in order to satisfy the *Bruen* standard. As a result, the Court concluded that the nation's "tradition of firearm regulation allows the Government to disarm individuals who present a credible threat to the physical safety of others."[12]

The Concurrences and Dissents

While Chief Justice Roberts' relatively brief majority opinion was joined by eight of the nine justices, the case generated no fewer than five separate concurring opinions. Two of the concurring opinions, from Justices Jackson and Sotomayor (joined by Justice Kagan) took the position that *Bruen* was wrongly decided, criticizing its "myopic focus on history

---

[8] *Rahimi*, slip op. at 7.
[9] *Id*.
[10] *Id*.
[11] *Id*. at 13.
[12] *Id*. at 16.

and tradition"[13] and describing post-*Bruen* case law applying the "historical tradition" standard as "'increasingly erratic and unprincipled.'"[14] Justice Sotomayor also highlighted social science data on the prevalence of intimate partner violence, data that is notably absent from the majority opinion and rendered largely irrelevant under the *Bruen* standard.[15] Three of the concurrences came from justices who had joined the *Bruen* majority: Justices Kavanaugh, Gorsuch, and Barrett. Each used their opinions to endorse the broader use of history to interpret the Second Amendment and to reject alternative approaches that would give greater weight to the government's interest in combatting gun violence.

It is notable that Justice Thomas, the author of *Bruen* (and therefore presumably the justice most qualified to opine on its meaning) was the lone dissenter in *Rahimi*. Thomas' primary source of disagreement was with the majority's choice of historical analogues. He characterized the Second Amendment as a direct response to overly restrictive disarmament authority wielded by the Crown during the 1600 s, and argued that §922(g)(8) was significantly broader in scope than the analogues cited by the majority, and therefore failed the "historical tradition" test. Thomas noted that the government disarmed Rahimi even though he had never been convicted of a crime, and that the state could have used criminal prosecution for aggravated assault to effectively disarm Rahimi and other dangerous persons.

RAHIMI'S IMPLICATIONS

Rahimi will likely emerge as a relatively minor chapter in the Roberts' Court's dramatic move toward originalist methodology in many areas of constitutional law, including the Second Amendment. Indeed, the case is most notable for what it leaves unresolved.

With regard to the "historical tradition" standard, while *Rahimi* suggests that lower courts should look to larger "principles" rather than a "historical twin," the case does not offer much additional guidance for lower courts struggling with how to divine those principles, what constitutes sufficient evidence of those principles, the level of weight that

---

[13] *Id*. at 5 (Sotomayor, J., concurring).

[14] *Id*. at 5 (Jackson, J., concurring).

[15] *Id*. at 5–6 (Sotomayor, J., concurring).

should be given to different historical sources, or what level of abstraction courts should apply when reviewing the suitability of historical analogues. It also fails to resolve the role of post-ratification historical evidence, including historical traditions that involve the time period surrounding Reconstruction.

Moreover, *Rahimi* makes it unclear how the Second Amendment might apply to other regulations that disarm potentially dangerous persons, like federal laws that prohibit certain persons convicted of non-violent felonies from possessing a gun. On one hand, *Rahimi* contains a strong statement that will likely appear in subsequent lower court opinions, affirming that the nation's "tradition of firearm regulation allows the Government to disarm individuals who present a credible threat to the physical safety of others."[16] It also noted language from *Heller* stating that prohibitions on firearms possession by persons who have been convicted of felonies or are mentally ill are "presumptively lawful."[17]

On the other hand, *Rahimi* specifically highlighted the procedural protections and limited scope of §922(g)(8): the law only applies to situations where a judge has found that an individual presents "a credible threat to the physical safety" of another person and that the disarmament provision is limited in time (it only applies for as long as a person is subject to a restraining order).[18] This might provide lower courts with a basis for distinguishing *Rahimi* from other firearms restrictions on dangerous persons that have wider application or lack similar procedural safeguards.

It also leaves open questions about exactly who is qualified to assess whether a person represents a threat to public safety, or what standards that person is required to use when making that determination.

In short, despite placing some constraints on the application of *Bruen*, it is hard to see *Rahimi* as a game-changer for Second Amendment doctrine. Originalism remains the predominant interpretive paradigm, *Bruen*'s central approach remains intact, the government continues to bear the burden of proof when defending firearms regulations, and an obsessive focus on historical analogues continues to be an essential component of Second Amendment litigation. Lower court judges that were looking to *Rahimi* to provide greater clarity on how to resolve

---

[16] *Rahimi*, slip op. at 16.
[17] *Id.* at 15.
[18] *Id.* at 14.

Second Amendment challenges to other firearms regulations are likely to be disappointed and will need to wait for further elaboration from the Court.

CHAPTER 15

Alexander v. South Carolina State Conference of the NAACP: A Political Exception to the Rule Against Race-Based Redistricting

Mark R. Killenbeck

What role may race play in the decennial process of drawing district lines for federal and state elections? In *Alexander v. South Carolina Conference of the NAACP*,[1] the Court held that a congressional districting map was not an impermissible exercise in racial gerrymandering. The map in question was adopted by a Republican-controlled legislature that wished to create a stronger Republican "tilt" in one of the two districts in the Charleston, South Carolina area. That required significant movement of the black voting age population (BVAP) in an attempt to preserve Democratic influence in an adjoining district. Both the individual charged with drawing the map and the legislature understood that in South Carolina there was a strong correlation between race and party affiliation and support, with the BVAP skewing sharply in favor of the Democrats. They

[1] 144 S. Ct. 1221 (2024).

M. R. Killenbeck (✉)
University of Arkansas School of Law, Fayetteville, NC, USA
e-mail: mkillenb@uark.edu

believed, accordingly, that they were undertaking a permissible exercise of the traditional state power to engage in partisan gerrymandering.

The NAACP and an individual voter challenged the map, arguing that it was in fact a racial gerrymander that diluted the electoral power of black voters. A three-judge district court held that the map violated the Equal Protection Clause of the Fourteenth Amendment and barred use of the map until it was presented with and approved a new map. The state appealed, filing directly with the Supreme Court, as is the norm in such cases under special jurisdictional rules. The Court noted probable jurisdiction, heard the appeal, held for the state, and remanded the case for further proceedings in accordance with its ruling.

Writing for himself, Chief Justice Roberts and Justices Thomas, Gorsuch, Kavanaugh, and Barrett, Justice Alito declared that "[t]he fact of the matter is that politics pervaded the highly visible mapmaking process from start to finish."[2] The challengers accordingly failed to meet the applicable burden, which requires a showing of a "'purposeful device to minimize or cancel out the voting potential of racial or ethnic minorities.'"[3] Justice Thomas filed a concurring opinion, agreeing with the result but arguing that the Court should return to the rule that cases of this sort should not be heard by the courts. Justice Kagan, joined by Justice Sotomayor and Jackson, dissented, maintaining that the state "exploit[ed] the well-known correlation between race and voting behavior,"[4] and that "partisanship subsumed race in the design of" the districts.[5]

Background Principles: Constitutional Limits on Redistricting

In the wake of each decennial census, district lines are reexamined and, where necessary, redrawn to reflect changing demographics. The controlling consideration is the "one person, one vote" principle, a rule adopted by the Supreme Court in a series of cases, including *Baker v. Carr*,[6]

---

[2] *Id.* at 1244.

[3] *Id.* at 1252 (quoting *Miller v. Johnson*, 515 U.S. 900, 911 [1995]).

[4] *Alexander*, 144 S. Ct. at 1268.

[5] *Id.* at 1285.

[6] 369 U.S. 186 (1962).

Reynolds v. Sims,[7] and *Wesberry v. Sanders*.[8] That doctrine seeks to ensure that each individual is treated equally as to their voting power and, with certain limited exceptions, requires that legislative districts have roughly equal populations. To use a crude example, if a state has one million citizens and ten electoral districts, the expectation would be that each district would have a population of one hundred thousand individuals.

Prior to *Baker*, these matters were treated as a nonjusticiable political question. In the leading case of *Colgrove v. Green*,[9] the Court found that "the history of... apportionment is its embroilment in politics, in the sense of party contests and party interests."[10] It recognized that "the most glaring disparities have prevailed as to the contours and the population of districts."[11] But it believed that the power to correct these manifest injustices lay with Congress and the states, and the "[c]ourts ought not enter into this political thicket."[12]

Baker and its progeny changed this understanding. There is a "basic standard of equality among voters,"[13] and that rule is violated when an individual's vote "is in a substantial fashion diluted when compared with votes of citizens living in other parts of the State."[14] That said, while the goal is a degree of mathematical precision in drawing lines, there are certain core principles that control and that may lead to exceptions. As the Court observed in *Karcher v. Daggett*, assuming "a good faith effort to achieve population equality . . . any number of consistently applied legislative policies might justify some variance, including, for instance, making districts compact, respecting municipal boundaries, preserving the core of prior districts, and avoiding contests between incumbent Representatives."[15]

It is important to understand, as the Court conceded in *Alexander*, that the Court has always recognized that,

---

[7] 377 U.S. 533 (1964).
[8] 376 U.S. 1 (1964).
[9] 328 U.S. 549 (1946).
[10] *Id.* at 555.
[11] *Id.*
[12] *Id.* at 556.
[13] *Id.* at 561.
[14] *Id.* at 568.
[15] 462 U.S. 725, 740 (1983).

redistricting is an inescapably political enterprise. Legislatures are almost always aware of the political ramifications of the maps they adopt, and claims that a map is unconstitutional because it was drawn to achieve a partisan end are not justiciable in federal court. Thus, as far as the Federal Constitution is concerned, a legislature may pursue partisan ends when it engages in redistricting.[16]

This is the *constitutional* standard and one of the key realities is that, as litigated, *Alexander* posed only constitutional questions triggered by the Equal Protection Clause of the Fourteenth Amendment. There are a second set of considerations raised by the statutory regime created by the Voting Rights Act of 1965 (VRA),[17] which declared that "[n]o voting qualification or prerequisite to voting, or standard, practice, or procedure shall be imposed or applied by any State or political subdivision to deny or abridge the right of any citizen of the United States to vote on account of race or color."[18] As the Court noted in *Abbott v. Perez*,[19] while "the Equal Protection Clause restricts the consideration of race in the districting process, compliance with the [VRA] pulls in the opposite direction: It often insists that districts be created precisely because of race" given its demand that a "districting plan [cannot] provide[] 'less opportunity' for racial minorities 'to elect representatives of their choice.'"[20]

That complicating factor was not present in *Alexander*. The sole issue for the Court was whether "'race for its own sake, and not other districting principles, was the legislature's dominant and controlling rationale in drawing its district lines.'"[21] The key consideration: whether "race predominated in the drawing of a district 'regardless of the motivations' for the use of race."[22] Consistent with the admonition that the "'mere

---

[16] *Alexander*, 144 S. Ct. 1233.

[17] Pub. L. 89–110, 79 Stat. 437 (1965).

[18] *Id.* § 2.

[19] 585 U.S. 579 (2018).

[20] *Id.* at 587 (quoting *League of United Latin American Citizens v. Perry*, 548 U.S. 399, 425 [2006]).

[21] *Alexander*, 144 S. Ct. at 1236 (quoting *Miller v. Johnson*, 515.S. 900, 913 [1995]).

[22] *Id.* at 1252 (quoting Shaw v. Reno, 509 U.S. 630, 645 [1993]).

use'" of race in such matters is at least suspect, if not barred,[23] "[t]he racial classification itself is the relevant harm in that context."[24]

The Ruling in the Case: Politics, Not Race

There was, Justice Alito wrote for the Court in *Alexander*, ample evidence in the record that political considerations played an important role in the process of both drawing and adopting the map at issue. Testimony at trial stressed that "partisanship was 'one of the most important factors' in the process and that the Republican Party was 'not going to pass a plan that sacrificed [District 1.'"[25] Traditional race-neutral districting criteria would be "honored."[26] But "the legislature's adoption of any map that improved the Democrats' chance of reclaiming District 1 would constitute 'political malpractice.'"[27]

That carried the day. The challengers were unable to "disentangle race and politics."[28] Given the presumption that the legislature acted in good faith, and the strong correlation between race and politics in a state where the BVAP overwhelmingly supported the Democrats, the Court was unwilling to side with the challengers. "'Our prior decisions have made clear that a jurisdiction may engage in constitutional political gerrymandering, even if it so happens that the most loyal Democrats happen to be black Democrats and even if the State were *conscious* of that fact.'"[29]

Justice Thomas filed a concurring opinion, writing that "[t]he Court correctly concludes that the judgment below must be reversed under our precedents."[30] He felt compelled to speak separately, however, to express his strong disagreement with those precedents. "Drawing political districts," he wrote, "is a task for politicians, not judges. There are no judicially manageable standards for resolving claim about redistricting,

---

[23] *Id.* at 1262 (citing *Bethune-Hill v. Virginia Board of Electors*, 580 U.S. [], 189 [2016]).

[24] *Id.* at 1252.

[25] *Id.* at 1237 (quoting Senate Majority Leader Shane Massey).

[26] *Id.*

[27] *Id.* (quoting Shane Massey).

[28] *Id.* at 1233.

[29] *Id.* at 1235 (quoting *Hunt v. Cromartie*, 526 U.S. 541,551 [1999]).

[30] *Id.* at 1252 (Thomas, J., concurring).

and, regardless, the Constitution commits these issues exclusively to the political branches."[31] More fundamentally, to do so was to "indulge in race-based reasoning inimical to the Constitution. As we reiterated last Term, '[o]ur Constitution is color-blind.'"[32]

Justice Kagan, writing for herself and Justices Sotomayor and Jackson, dissented. Characterizing the case as "a quintessential factual dispute,"[33] she stressed that the three-judge court that heard the case conducted a protracted and exhaustive review of a massive factual record and, "[f]aced with that proof, all three judges agreed: The Challengers version of the events was the most credible. The court, to put the matter bluntly, did not believe the state officials. It thought they had gerrymandered District 1 by race."[34] She recognized that the Court had held that partisan gerrymandering cases are not justiciable in *Rucho v. Common Cause*.[35] Stressing that "[t]he Framers were aware of electoral districting problems and considered what to do about them" the Court declared in *Rucho* that "[t]hey settled on a characteristic approach, assigning the issue to the state legislatures, expressly checked an balanced by the Federal Congress."[36]

Justice Kagan conceded that if in fact the state had simply "'targeted people who voted Democratic' from one district to another, its actions (however unsavory and undemocratic) are immune from federal constitutional challenge."[37] But she argued at length that the record did not support that conclusion and that the three-judge court, which was in the best position to assess the facts—and which under the Court's precedents was the entity to do so—properly concluded that the state was simply not telling the truth.

---

[31] *Id*. at 1253 (Thomas, J., concurring).

[32] *Id*. (quoting *Students for Fair Admissions, Inc. v. President and Fellows of Harvard College*, 600 U.S. 181, 230 [2023] (quoting *Plessy v. Ferguson*, 163 U.S. 537, 559 [1896] [Harlan, J., dissenting]).

[33] *Id*. at 1268 (Kagan, J., dissenting).

[34] *Id*. at 1268–69 (Kagan, J., dissenting).

[35] 139 S. Ct. 2482 (2019).

[36] *Id*. at [ ].

[37] *Alexander*, 144 S. Ct. at 1268 (Kagan, J., dissenting).

Implications of the Ruling for Future Cases

Alexander raises the bar for those wishing to challenge district lines as impermissible racial gerrymanders. Such claims remain justiciable, Justice Thomas notwithstanding, but will now be much more difficult to prove. Individuals wishing to make out a claim are almost certainly going to be required to mine the record and find direct evidence that "race for its own sake" was the dispositive consideration. Mere inferences or circumstantial evidence will not suffice. That may be easy in situations where, as they are wont to do, politicians speak first and think later. But, forewarned by Alexander, the professionals who in most circumstances bear the primary responsibility for drawing the maps will presumably proceed with care.

These are matters of no small importance in our current highly polarized political environment. The correlation between race and party affiliation in South Carolina is largely replicated throughout the nation. As the Court noted in *Alexander*, "[e]xit polls found that at least 90% of black voters voted for the Democratic candidate in South Carolina and throughout the Nation."[38] These divisions will persist, if not intensify, in the wake of a 2024 electoral cycle where the choices presented by the two parties at the national level were stark and for all practical matters irreconcilable.

That said, for better or worse, the district lines under which succeeding elections will be conducted have been drawn and will likely remain in place until the next census in 2030. In a similar vein, the core rules for districting set out in *Karcher* are still in place, as are the countervailing demands imposed by the VRA. As the Court stressed, "[w]e have noted that a State's partisan-gerrymandering defense . . . raises 'special challenges' for plaintiffs. To prevail, a plaintiff must 'disentangle race from politics' by proving 'that the former *drove* a district's lines.'"[39] The racial element must be clear and definitive, which "means, among other things, ruling out the competing explanation that political considerations dominated the legislature's redistricting efforts. If either politics or race could explain a district's contours, the plaintiff has not cleared the bar."[40]

It remains to be seen what lessons those who oversee such matters will draw from *Alexander*. State officials who are able to free themselves

---

[38] *Id.* at 1235.
[39] *Alexander*, 144 S. Cit. at 1235 (quoting *Cooper*, 581 U.S. at 308).
[40] *Id.*

from the demands of politicians interested only in their own partisan ends will presumably act with greater care. And, as Justice Thomas noted, Congress has the ability to address these matters.[41] As currently configured, however, it is unlikely that any plan that might make it out of the House of Representatives will pass muster in the Senate. That almost certainly consigns these matters to the states, which magnifies the stakes in what "is inescapably a political enterprise,"[42] entrusting these matters to individuals for whom partisan ends are the defining objective. All of which makes it unlikely that *Alexander* will prove to be the end of the story in these matters.

---

[41] *Id.* at 1259 (the Constitution "commits supervisory authority over congressional distr8cting to Congress alone") (Thomas, J. concurring).

[42] *Id.* at 1233.

CHAPTER 16

City of Grants Pass v. Johnson, et al.: Homelessness and the Eighth Amendment

William Rose

On June 28, 2024, in one of its final cases from the 2023 term, the U.S. Supreme Court announced its decision in *City of Grants Pass v. Johnson*.[1] In a 6–3 vote, with the justices divided along ideological lines, the Court held that the Eighth Amendment's Cruel and Unusual Punishments Clause does not restrain governments from using criminal penalties to police inhabitants of homeless encampments. Justice Gorsuch authored the majority opinion; the decision also produced a very brief concurrence from Justice Thomas, and a stinging dissent from Justice Sotomayor which was joined by Justices Kagan and Jackson. Informed by more than 80 *amicus* briefs (from which both the majority and dissenting opinions drew heavily), Gorsuch and Sotomayor often seemed in direct conversation with one another. The meaning and reach of the Eighth Amendment's "Cruel and Unusual Punishments" Clause was contested interpretive terrain for the Court, but so too were questions related to the

[1] 603 U.S. ___ 2024, No. 23-175, June 28, 2024.

W. Rose (✉)
Department of Political Science, Albion College, Albion, USA
e-mail: wrose@albion.edu

proper role of the courts in our democratic practices, how best to protect the interests of vulnerable populations from majoritarian overreach, and basic principles of federalism.

Background

According to the most recent "Point-in-Time Estimates" from the U.S. Department of Housing and Urban Development (HUD), "more than 650,000 people were experiencing homelessness on a single night in January 2023, *a 12% increase from 2022*" (emphasis added). The HUD Report also noted that "[t]he rise in homelessness at the beginning of 2023 continued a pre-pandemic trend from 2016 to 2020, when homelessness also increased."[2] Unsurprisingly, Petitioner and Respondents agreed that the growing number of people in the U.S. who are unhoused or unsheltered poses an increasingly difficult social problem to contend with, one that is most certainly national in scope, but a problem that especially manifests itself regionally—where the top five states with the highest rates of homelessness are all in the western U.S. (California, Oregon, Hawaii, Arizona, and Nevada).

Petitioner and Respondent also were in agreement on one further point: that the causes of homelessness are many and identifying and targeting them for more efficacious policy interventions is an enormously complex, but necessary, task. Citing to U.S. government numbers, Justice Gorsuch observed that homelessness in this country has reached its highest levels since the government began reporting data on the subject in 2007."[3] Indeed, "[s]ome suggest that homelessness may be the defining public health and safety crisis in the western U.S. today."[4]

State and local governments across the U.S. have struggled to find a workable balance of competing interests in this policy context. The question is what "tools" from the policy toolbox may state and local governments deploy to deal with this policy problem? Will they be a limited set of tools, with certain others being denied to government officials for constitutional reasons? Or would policy makers, both state

---

[2] Point-in-Time estimates are an "Annual Snapshot of the Number of Individuals in Shelters, Temporary Housing, and in Unsheltered Settings." HUD Press Release, Dec. 15, 2023.

[3] *City of Grant's Pass*, slip op. p. 2 (Gorsuch, J.).

[4] *Id.*

and local, have nearly complete freedom to pull from the toolbox those tools thought best for the job at hand? With the problem of homelessness being especially acute in the western U.S., it is perhaps both fitting, and inevitable, that the Ninth Circuit was the first federal circuit to fully engage this problem. In 2018, in *Martin v. City of Boise*, the Ninth Circuit considered whether "the Eighth Amendment's prohibition on cruel and unusual punishment bars a city from prosecuting people criminally for sleeping outside on public property when those people have no home or other shelter to go to."[5] The Court concluded that it did. At issue was the constitutionality of two city ordinances from Boise, Idaho.

Struggling to respond to the growing number of homeless persons on its city streets and sidewalks, Boise passed a "Camping Ordinance,"[6] that made it a misdemeanor criminal offense to use "any of the streets, sidewalks, parks, or public places as a camping place at any time." Additionally, the City passed a "Disorderly Conduct Ordinance" that banned "[o]ccupying, lodging, or sleeping in any building, structure, or public place, whether public or private… without the permission of the owner…."[7]

Both ordinances represented a core part of what might be characterized as a "carrot and stick" approach by the Boise City Council, ostensibly intended to ease the pressures of an increasing homeless population on public spaces within the city. Viewed sympathetically, the city of Boise had merely sought to populate its policy toolbox with a range of tools to be deployed at its discretion, as the situation warranted, including the use of criminal sanctions. However, six current or former Boise residents who were or had been homeless challenged the lawfulness of the ordinances, alleging that they (the current and former residents) had been cited by Boise police for violating one or both of the ordinances. The plaintiffs sought both retrospective and prospective relief, the latter in the form of a permanent injunction enjoining the city of Boise from enforcing the ordinances against the plaintiffs and all those similarly situated—what would come to be referred to in Justice Gorsuch's majority opinion in *City of*

---

[5] *Martin v. City of Boise*, 902 F.3d 1031 (9th Cir., 2018).

[6] Boise City Code, sec. 9-10-02.

[7] Boise City Code, sec. 6-01-05.

Grants Pass as "*Martin* injunctions," and more derisively as the "*Martin* experiment."[8]

In reaching a decision largely supportive of the *Martin* plaintiffs' claims, the Ninth Circuit panel was clearly impressed by the practical problem of the mismatch between the numbers of homeless and unsheltered people in Boise on any given night and the number of shelter beds available. According to the 2016 "Point-in-Time Count" (*PIT Count*),[9] the city of Boise and surrounding Ada County had an estimated 867 homeless individuals, with 125 being fully unsheltered. In Boise's three homeless shelters combined there were a total of 354 beds available, supplemented by 92 "overflow" mats. The question, then, was this: did the city, at its own discretion, have a right to enforce its public sleeping and camping bans, using citations and fines—and deploying this approach as one possible "tool" among many—when there was no other available place for the homeless to sleep? In other words, could the city punish such individuals for being unhoused and unsheltered, thus creating a status offense of homelessness? The *Martin* three-judge panel concluded the answer was "no"; relying on *Robinson v. California*[10] the court held that "an ordinance violates the Eighth Amendment's 'Cruel and Unusual Punishments Clause' insofar as it imposes criminal sanctions against homeless individuals for [involuntarily] sleeping outdoors, on public property, when no alternative shelter is available to them."[11]

THE MAJORITY OPINION

The city of Grants Pass sits in the southwest region of Oregon. It has a population of approximately 38,000 and it has a homeless population of roughly 600 individuals. At the time that this litigation took place, Grants

---

[8] *City of Grant's Pass*, slip op. at 8 (Gorsuch, J.).

[9] Conducted by the Idaho Housing and Finance Association in the last year before the commencement of the *Martin* litigation.

[10] 370 U.S. 660 (1962). *Robinson* drew a clear distinction between status and conduct, and held that it was constitutionally impermissible for someone to be punished for a status offense; in *Robinson*, the petitioner had been convicted in state court for the status of being addicted to drugs in violation of a California statute that criminalized drug addiction.

[11] *Id.*, at 1035.

Pass had one homeless facility—the Gospel Rescue Mission—a Christian-based shelter that imposed both work and religious worship requirements to qualify for a bed. In addition, there were time constraints, limiting the total number of days a homeless person might seek refuge there. For those who qualified, the Gospel Rescue Mission had 138 beds.

In an effort to address its homelessness problems, the city of Grants Pass adopted three ordinances that were related to conduct associated with homelessness: public sleeping and encampments in public spaces. The first ordinance prohibited sleeping "on public sidewalks, streets, or alleyways at any time as a matter of individual and public safety."[12] The second ordinance prohibited "[c]amping on any sidewalk, street...or any other publicly-owned property...."[13] The final ordinance addressed the use of public parks, prohibiting camping in all city parks. The ordinances were enforced by civil fines that increased with repeated violations. Repeat offenders of the ban on camping in public parks were also subject to 30-day bans from access to the parks. Violators of the park ban would then be considered to have violated criminal trespass regulations, and be subject to a jail sentence of up to 30 days. Arguing that they had a credible fear of criminal sanction, three homeless persons, who were also long-term residents of Grants Pass, successfully challenged the enforcement of the public sleeping and public camping ordinances in the lower federal courts. Relying on Eighth Amendment arguments from *Martin*, the plaintiffs successfully argued that the Cruel and Unusual Punishments Clause precluded the imposition of criminal penalties where, as here, with no shelter beds available, plaintiffs slept and/or camped on public property.

A six-member majority rejected the plaintiffs' (Respondents') Eighth Amendment arguments and effectively overturned *Martin*. Writing for the majority, Justice Gorsuch was clear: "[W]e discern nothing in the Eighth Amendment that might provide us with lawful authority to extend *Robinson* beyond its narrow holding."[14] According to Gorsuch, "the city's laws parallel those found in countless jurisdictions across the country. And because laws like these do not criminalize mere status,

---

[12] Grants Pass Municipal Code, Sec. 5.61.020 (A).

[13] Grants Pass Municipal Code, Sec. 5.61.030.

[14] *City of Grant's Pass* slip op. at 23 (Gorsuch, J.).

Robinson is not implicated."[15] The city ordinances are not *cruel*, Gorsuch said, "because none is designed to 'superad[d] terror, pain, or disgrace.'" "Nor are the city's sanctions unusual, because similar punishment has been" commonly used by city governments throughout the country.[16] Resisting the call to extend *Robinson* to meet the circumstances present in Grants Pass, Gorsuch observed instead that the *Robinson* Court "expressly recognized the 'broad power' States enjoy over the substance of their criminal laws."[17]

Such deference to state and local political authorities runs throughout the majority's argument. Roughly the first third of Gorsuch's opinion speaks to the desirability of giving local political leaders access to the full "toolbox", providing them with the flexibility to make democratically accountable decisions about how best to respond to the many challenges posed by growing homeless populations. Drawing heavily from *amicus* briefs filed by state and local government entities or their political allies, Gorsuch champions the need to enhance local governmental autonomy, while simultaneously recognizing a limited role for the courts—it is a policy problem best entrusted to the political branches of government. Indeed, Gorsuch resisted the claims of a mismatch between available shelter beds and the demands by homeless persons for one of the beds. Instead, Gorsuch argued that the real problem was a lack of use of available beds. For a variety of reasons, many within homeless populations, in Grants Pass and elsewhere, simply refused to go into the shelters. With *Martin* in place, providing legal cover for the choice to remain on the streets, cities were unable to rely upon the coercive "stick" of criminal sanction to help move homeless persons from public spaces into shelters. With *Martin* gone, cities have greater freedom to develop and deploy more workable solutions.

THE DISSENTING OPINION

Justice Sotomayor submitted a vigorous dissent, arguing that the majority opinion misreads and mis-applies *Robinson;* that if it does not control this case by its own terms it can be, and should be, extended to do

---

[15] *Id.*, at 21.
[16] *Id.*, at 17.
[17] *Id.*, at 20.

so. Several times during oral argument, Sotomayor insisted that Grants Pass was seeking to punish individuals for engaging in a basic human function—sleeping.[18] The sleeping ban and the camping ban sought to regulate behavior that was, in essence, involuntary; that is, the very condition of being homeless places one in a position where they cannot help but do what the law otherwise forbids. For Sotomayor, *Robinson* spoke directly to the real issue at hand. While the Grants Pass ordinances may not have proscribed "status" as such, they did sanction conduct that homeless persons (when shelter beds were unavailable) could not help but engage in. To ignore this point, said Sotomayor, allows the city to punish someone because of their status—and this, *Robinson* clearly prohibits.

Conclusions

For cities in the Ninth Circuit and elsewhere in the near term, they will again be able to enforce legal bans on certain conduct (e.g., public sleeping and public camping bans), should they choose to do so. In the longer term, they will have the flexibility to experiment, within reasonable limits, with viable approaches to balancing competing interests in the use of their public spaces. For those who are unhoused and unsheltered, a precarious existence may have become slightly more so. Though both the dissenting and majority opinions recognized and articulated other legal recourse that homeless persons may make use of to protect their interests.

---

18 https://www.oyez.org/cases/2023/23-175.

Index

A
Abbott v. Perez, 144
Abortion, 2, 5, 12, 18, 50–56
  medical abortion, 39, 47
Administrative adjudication, 68, 70, 71, 73
Administrative law, 76
Administrative Law Judge (ALJ), 65, 66, 73
Administrative Procedure Act (APA), 42
Administrative Procedure Act of 1946 (APA), 79
Administrative rulemaking, 79, 84
Agency, federal, 8
Alexander v. South Carolina Conference of the NAACP, 141
Alito, Samuel, 2, 3, 8, 43
Alliance for Hippocratic Medicine, 39
Amicus briefs, 149, 154
Appropriation, 57, 59–64
Appropriations Clause, 58–64
Arbitrary and capricious, 91
Arbitrary or capricious, 89

Article III, 73
Article III court, 68
Article III, duty of courts, 79
Atlas Roofing, 69–73
Aunt Bertha v. NLRB, 4

B
Baker v. Carr, 142
Balkin, Jack, 4
Bantam Book, Inc. v. Sullivan, 116–119
Barrett, Amy Coney, 26, 128
Berger, Victor, 22
Bethune-Hill v. Virginia Board of Electors, 580 U.S. [], 189 (2016), 145
Biden v. Nebraska, 5
Biden v. Nebraska, 600 U.S. 477 (2023), 46
Brown v. Board of Education, 24
Bruen, 134–139

C

Chevron, 92, 93
Chevron deference [also judicial deference], 76, 77, 79, 80, 83
Chevron U.S.A. v. Natural Resources Defense Council, 76
Chief Justice Roberts, 53
Church Amendments, 44
Civil penalties, 65, 67–73
Clean Air Act, 76, 77, 84
Clean Air Act of 1970, 88, 91
Clean Power Plan, 77
Clean Water Act, 84
Coercion, 115, 118, 120, 121
Colgrove v. Green, 143
Color of law, 125, 127
Commerce Clause, 25
Common law, 66, 67, 69, 70, 72, 73
Comstock Law, 47
Confidence, in Supreme Court, 3
Congress, 21–23, 26, 28, 92
Congress, delegation of discretionary authority to agencies, 81
Conscience protection statutes, 40, 45
Constitution of the United States, 21
Consumer Financial Protection Bureau, 58
Criminal prosecution, 29–32, 36, 37
Cruel and Unusual Punishments Clause, 149, 152, 153
Cyberspace, 96, 100

D

Democrats, 28
Dept. of Health and Human Services, 45
District of Columbia v. Heller, 134
Dobbs v. Jackson Women's Health Organization (2022), 4, 50
Dual for-cause removal, 66
Due Process Clause, 3

E

Eighth Amendment, 149, 151–153
Eisenstadt v. Baird, 50
Election fraud, 29, 31
Electronic amplification, 110, 111
Enumerated powers, 61
Environmental Protection Agency (EPA), 83, 87–92
Environmental regulations, 75
Equal Protection Clause, 142
Equal Protection Clause of the Fourteenth Amendment, 144
Establishment Clause, 4
Expenditure, 59

F

Facebook, 96, 123, 126, 127, 129
Federal Emergency Medical Treatment and Labor Act (EMTALA), 51, 53–55
Federalism, 25, 26, 150
Federal Reserve, 59
First Amendment, 4, 6, 7, 9, 15, 16, 19, 95, 96, 98, 100, 101, 115–117, 120, 121, 123–128, 130, 131
  censorship, 106
  disfavored speech, 105, 106
  free speech, 106, 109, 112
Food & Drug Administration (FDA), 39, 40, 42, 46, 47
Food & Drug Admin. v. All. for Hippocratic Med., 602 U.S. 367 (2024), 40, 46
Foreign influence operations, 109, 111
  election interference, 112
Foreign propaganda
  China, 109, 111
  Iran, 109, 111
  North korea, 111
  Russia, 109, 111

Forgotten Fourteenth Amendment, 22
Fourteenth Amendment, 3, 21, 23–25, 142
Fourteenth Amendment, Section 3, 22, 23, 25, 28
Fraud, 65–67, 69, 71, 72
Freedom of speech, 15
Free Speech, 115–118, 120

G

Gerrymandering, 141
Glorious Revolution, 60
Gorsuch, Neil, 27, 43
Gospel Rescue Mission, 153
Griswold v. Connecticut, 50

H

Healthcare desert, 45
Heller, 134, 135
Historical tradition, 135–138
Homeless, rights of, 10, 17
House of Representatives, 22
Hunt v. Cromartie, 526 U.S. 541,551 (1999), 145

I

Idaho v. U.S., 49
Information warfare, 112

J

January 6, 2021 insurrection, 22, 24
Jarkesy, George, 65, 66, 69–72
Judicial restraint, 76
June Med. Servs. L.L.C. v. Russo, 591 U.S. 299 (2020), 43
Jury, 66, 71–73
Jury trial, right to, 14
Justice Alito, 53, 55, 142
Justice Barrett, 53–55, 66, 142
Justice Gorsuch, Neil, 53–55, 66, 69, 70, 72, 73, 120, 142, 149–151, 153, 154
Justice Jackson, Kentanji Brown, 26, 52–54, 120, 142, 149
Justice Kagan, Elena, 26, 52–55, 142, 149
Justice Kavanaugh, 53, 66, 142
Justice Roberts, 142
Justices Alito, 66
Justice Sotomayor, Sonia, 2, 7–10, 18, 26, 52–55, 70, 71, 119, 142, 149, 154
Justice Thomas, Clarence, 53, 55, 66, 72, 73, 142, 149

K

Karcher v. Daggett, 143
Kavanaugh, Brett, 39
Kennedy v. Bremerton School District, 4

L

Legislative history, 45
Lindke v. Freed, 124, 126–130
Lithwick, Dahlia, 2
Lochner v. New York, 101
Loper Bright Enterprises, 93

M

Magnuson-Stevens Fishery Conservation and Management Act of 1976 [or Magnuson-Stevens Act(MSA)], 77
Major questions doctrine, 77, 92
Marietta, Morgan, 5, 12, 13, 15–17
Marketplace of ideas, 96, 98–100, 102, 103
Martin injunctions, 152

Martin v. City of Boise, 151
Medical misinformation, 110, 111, 113
   COVID-19, 108, 109, 112
Miami Herald Publishing Co. v. Tornillo, 97
Mifepristone, 39, 40, 42, 44, 47
Miller v. Johnson, 515 .S. 900, 913 (1995), 144
Missouri Higher Education Loan Authority (MOHELA), 46
Moral beliefs, 41
Motion to dismiss, 118, 121
Moyle v. United States, 6, 12, 49

N

National Association for the Advancement of Colored People (NAACP), 142
National Marine Fisheries Service (NMFS), 77, 78, 83
National Rifle Association (NRA), 116–121
National Rifle Association v. Vullo, 115, 118, 121
NetChoice, 95–98, 100, 103
New England Fishery Management Council, 77
New Mexico, 22, 24
New York State Rifle and Pistol Association v. Bruen (2022), 4, 134
New York Times, 25
Ninth Circuit, 151, 152, 155
Ninth Circuit Court of Appeals, 52
Nixon v. Fitzgerald, 30

O

O'Connor-Radcliff v. Garnier, 124, 126–129
Office of the United States, 24

Officer of the United States, 21, 24
"One person, one vote" principle, 142
Originalism, 134
Originalist, 138
Original public meaning, 59–62, 64
Overfishing, 77
Overton Window, 4

P

Packingham v. North Carolina, 100, 123–125
Parliament, 60, 62
Per curiam, 25, 26
Planned Parenthood v. Casey, 50
Plessy v. Ferguson, 146
"Point-in-Time Estimates", 150
Presidential immunity, 37
   civil, 37
   criminal, 37
Presidential power, 29, 31, 35, 37
   core, 31
   presumptive, 31
Presidents, 24
Private rights, 72
Pruneyard Shopping Center v. Robins, 99
Public employee, 125, 130
Public rights, 67, 68, 70–73

R

Racial gerrymander, 142
Rahimi, 134, 135
Rahimi, Zackey, 136–139
Reconstruction, 22, 24
Reconstruction Republicans, 26
Reproductive rights, 39, 40, 44, 46
Reynolds v. Sims, 143
Right of reproductive privacy, 50
Roberts Court, 1–3, 11, 13, 15, 17, 19
Roberts, John, 7, 25

Robinson v. California, 152
Roe v. Wade, 50, 51
Rucho v. Common Cause, 11, 17, 146

S

Second Amendment, 3–5, 16, 19, 133–139
Secretary of State, Maine, 25
Securities and Exchange Commission (SEC), 65–67, 69–73
Seventh Amendment, 66–71
Shaw v. Reno, 509 U.S. 630, 645 (1993), 144
Shelby County v. Holder, 17
Social media, 96, 97, 100, 101, 123, 124, 127–130
   ban users, 106
   content moderation, 107, 109
   Facebook, 105, 109, 112, 113
   Google, 113
   suspend users, 106
   warning labels, 105
   YouTube, 112
Source and purpose, 61
Standing, 5, 7, 12
   causation, 108
   injury, 107, 108
   redressability, 107
   third party standing, 42
Stare decisis, 80, 83
State action, 124, 125, 127–130
   Coercion, 107
   persuasion, 109
Statement and Account Clause, 59
Strict scrutiny, 124
Structural analysis, 64
Students for Fair Admissions, Inc. v. President and Fellows of Harvard College, 146
Suppression of expression, 116
Supreme Court of Colorado, 24

Supreme Court of the United States, 22
   Chief Justice Roberts, 31
   Justice Barrett, 34
   Justice Jackson, 35
   Justice Kagan, 35
   Justice Sotomayor, 35, 37
   Justice White, 30

T

Terrorism
   Christchurch call, 111
   terrorist content, 109–111
Thirteenth Amendment, 24
Thirty-Ninth Congress, 24
303 Creative v. Elenis, 5
Tingley v. Ferguson, 5
Total Abortion Ban, 50–52, 54, 55
Trump, Donald, 11, 22, 23, 28–31, 33–35, 38, 97
   presidency of, 22
Trump v. Anderson, 6, 8, 10, 11, 22, 23, 25–28
Trump v. United States, 6, 8, 10, 11, 29
Twitter, 97

U

Unconstitutional delegation of legislative power, 66
United States Department of Justice, 31, 32
United States v. Rahimi, 133
U.S. Department of Housing and Urban Development (HUD), 150

V

VanDerStok v. Garland, 5
Viability, 50

Vice president, 23
Vice President of the United States, 33, 35
Voting Rights Act of 1965 (VRA), 17, 144
Vullo, Maria, 118

W
Wesberry v. Sanders, 143
West Coast Hotel v. *Parrish*, 101
West Virginia v. EPA (2022), 4, 13, 77
World War One, 22